LETTERS
TO
ANGELA

Phillip D. Reisner

Speaking Beyond the
Horizon with Pending Letters

Writing

Words mind fall
like rain drops,
futile alone, but
grand in written sum,
thoughts then
become real and
ideas emerge as
paper placed
gathering storms.

Feelings flower and
disappear with
relenting beauty as
might delicate memories,
like surrendering clouds
evaporate with hot sun,
like love filled
clouds disappear with
careless mind.

Don't crush or
smash fragile
fleeting words, but
read them gently
within whole
composed candor,
for too soon night
consumes day and
mind goes black.

LETTERS TO

ANGELA

Trafford rev. 8/15/2011

 www.trafford.com

North America & international
toll-free: 1 888 232 4444 (USA & Canada)
phone: 250 383 6864 ♦ fax: 812 355 4082

Also by Phillip D. Reisner

Whispering
Time Remnants

PREFACE

This book provides intimate glimpses of my love for two daughters. I do this through undelivered, pending letters written from wonderful life memories shared and hurtful instigating actions endured. The letters concern nearly eighteen years of allotted time, energy and adoration. They express personal feelings concerning two of my daughters, and describe outside sources that alter life and threaten relationships. I write the letters during several months of soul searching and emotional venting. I reflect on spiritual and earthly forces that affect my life, beliefs and relationships.

I write about life and death, give and take, denial and acceptance. Sometimes reasoning is impossible and only faith is promising. I confirm each day that the sun does indeed come up again while pain and suffering threaten hope. Some things are unchangeable while other things require for and against fighting. Acceptance is a positive state of mind. Rejection is a negative earthly fight that is always difficult. I balance between acceptance and rejection while discovering middle ground through reasoning and understanding. I find solace only through faith. I yet wait for truth to surface.

I write about personal historical attempts to alienate me and my daughter, and finally actions that peak with horrible consequences. I believe that destructive forces can only shortly estrange me from my daughter. Sometimes it seems to be the devil's work as innocence succumbs to wickedness. This book demonstrates the repeated testing of my strength from the best to the worst that can happen. My strengths are vulnerable to subversion, but I do not succumb to those who wish to turn my strengths into weaknesses.

This book is about self-control and humility, love and joy. It is about a constant grasping for and the handling of tenuous time. I struggle against God's spiritual forces that strengthen me with love, and against the devil's evil forces trying to subvert my strengths with selfishness. I touch on parental alienation. I deal with how one parent attempts to steal another parent's rights. I barely touch on this subject, but share some strong feelings concerning it.

I try to protect feelings and reputations in this book by not telling the whole story. However, I do share enough feelings that seep from deep within to demonstrate personal hurt and disappointment.

It appears that life attempts to subvert my strengths into perceived weaknesses. Life measures my faith, steadfastness and love. Short-term faith seems successful, but perseverance seems not to pay off during the writing of these letters. I do, however, believe that patience will surely have its reward through faith and hope. Pain has its healing salve and injury its braces. Without pain, there is no gain, so "they" say. I believe that there is much gaining of knowledge in these letters. I also believe that there is possible opening of the heart and mind for the reader.

Without time, there is no process. Love is a painful process no matter the relationship. A parent is a parent for life and no one can take that away.

My poetry, although obtuse, further explains some of my deep feelings. Sometimes hidden truth is more obvious when viewed through an opaque window. Unspeakable thoughts and ideas are sometimes obtuse. A provoking mental mirror can reflect opinions and beliefs, sometimes best providing truth. Intellectual glass and silver, like a physical mirror, can reveal much through inner reflection.

I believe life is simpler than perceived, wisdom is more available than realized and finding answers can be as easy as picking low branch apples. It is the carrying around of answers, without a rational basket, that complicates life. Remedy control is a frustrating thing. Most solutions are from beginning to end, round like apples. Round solutions will not remain in place, and eventually they rot and stink. They need constant protecting and preserving.

There are no real solutions or answers, only illusions and pretentious ideas. Perhaps love and pain seem more real than anything does when it is personal. I think reality and understanding emerge in retrospect as one gains true perspective through time.

I am trying to gain perspective with these letters. Frankly, there are big and little heart attacks when considered in retrospect. Heart attacks come in all sizes and shapes. They can be either physical, mental or both. Eventually everyone has one. However, when one has experienced the worst, everything else is endurable. It is kind of like an immunization that falls short of comprehensive protection. It covers almost anything that can overwhelm, but just cannot help or prevent everything. Pain may subside, but scars remain forever. Grief may diminish, but memories endure eternally.

I think life is kind of like a graph with "x" being time and "y" being awareness. It begins and ends at zero, no matter how long one lives. Never does it display a smooth predictable line or a sweet smooth correctly allocated bell curve. Never is the curve a normal distribution of probabilities, but instead, it is a jagged volatile rise and fall of positive and negative experiences. Here in lies the crux of my letters, for my graph flows from melancholy to joyful, from injury to healing. I fear that I cannot show enough of my life curve for my daughter to understand the need to purge her heart, mind and soul. Her life curve has taken a sharp spike that needs attention.

My graph spikes and quickly stabilizes, all the while flowing towards a peak and then towards a valley of death. The letters and poems reveal a small sliver of my life curve. I have the jagged lifeline of a complex time traveler, but I am going nowhere. My lifeline curve represents diverse experiences gliding along a inevitable line as my ageing body unpredictably limps towards conclusion.

Life is unpredictable, and my mental heart attack was just around the next corner. A spike was hiding within my self controlled and easy flowing graph line, and I could not see or even imagine its dynamic arrival.

I yet meander through life, vacillating between known and unknown, and learn what knowledge enhances luck and success. I rely on ignorance and lack of propaganda while accepting the spiritual world in a child-like manner. I sit quietly recalling counsel. I walk slowly seeking direction. I pray humbly waiting protection. I sincerely write my experiences, beliefs and wisdom in pending letters to Angela.

Belief in evil exploration and faith in divine providence continue to test my resolve. I attempt to improve my short-term luck while learning that destiny is an uncontrollable mystery. I reason that fate and faith are spiritual things and all I can do is remain a loving father and pray.

CONTENTS

INTRODUCTION

Angela Lea is my daughter. She and her identical twin sister Kaitlyn Marie were born pre-mature on March 29, 1993. Kaitlyn died at age three and a half on September 28, 1996. She has another sister, Kristen, born in 1972 and a brother, Brook, born in 1970.

When I speak of the worst that can happen to a parent, I know about what I am talking. Then again, I see horrific stories in the news, tragic deaths of children by the hands of perverts and murderers. I see injury and disease taking young lives. I see hunger and poverty killing sweet innocent children. I have a better understanding of life now in retrospect.

My daughter Kaitlyn passed with dignity and grace. She died quickly and peacefully of septicemia from Streptopneumococis A bacteria, because she was born without a spleen and we did not know it. Kaitlyn's autopsy revealed this to be so and later we discovered that Angela also does not have a spleen.

I thought at the time of her death that maybe she was taken to heaven to not suffer future hardships. As it turns out, Angela has and is enduring much adversity in her life. I will reveal some of her hardships in these letters and poems. I shall reveal some of my own hardships and feelings in this book. I have no complaints. I am blessed. I had three and a half years with Kaitlyn, and Angela is yet alive. My other children are doing great and I have five wonderful healthy grand children. All of my children and grand-children are true blessings.

These are tough times for Angela who turns eighteen on March 29 of 2011. I have been in a position of little influence since her mother and I got a divorce. We did not have a sound marriage even before Kaitlyn's death, but had no resemblance of a marriage after her death. We never really touched or talked to each other after March 28, 1996. She went her way and I went my way. She healed her way and I healed my way. I cannot speak for her, but I found counsel in only one person, that being the Holy Spirit. My minister, good friends and writers of books could not help me understand why Kaitlyn passed. Only God through the Holy Spirit allowed me to accept truth through faith, and understanding through acceptance.

Life length is no measure of life quality. A perfect life can be lived shortly, but the odds for an imperfect life increases with time. Everything seems to decline immediately or at least shortly after human creation. Kaitlyn lived a perfect life, knowing nothing bad, hurtful or painful. I have gained a better understanding of God's life cycle through passing years. Time is no measure of success. Time, however, has been a friend of mine.

I hope Angela will someday find my words worthy of her time. I hope she finds understanding of self and solace in her soul. I pray that she will find truth and it will set her free.

These undelivered letters involve writing to Angela candidly with some heretofore-unexpressed feelings. They represent a small sliver of our lives together. I hope someday she will read them and they will help her mend our minds and hearts, and renew our relationship.

Therefore, I say, "here's to us." It is an expression and a toast we made with diet coke, lemonade and milk at dinnertime when Angela visited Debi and me, and made us a family.

CHAPTER I

Celestial Traveling

Celestial Path

She soared beyond stars and
planets to get here,
beyond Venus and
Milky Way.
She swam time seas and
climbed cosmos peaks.
She sought no place to be
except Earth and
in mortal loving arms.

She chose her life,
parents and consequences.
She chose lessons to
discover and
spirituality to gain.

Most is gone now, for
she can hardly remember
from where she came or
who sent her.

Faith carried her here and
faith will return her.
And, to think she came
with another, a
twin sister to lead way
into humanity and
self expression.
She shall soar again and
again until getting it right.

Dear Angela – *Scrapbooks*

I was looking at the scrapbooks we put together when you were younger. The earliest one is 1999 and the latest is 2008. I think they are so cool. I am not quite sure why we quit doing them. It was more than a passing interest for both of us that lasted nearly ten years. They document our time together when it was just you and me, and then later with Debi. They got me thinking about us, especially after June 16 when I talked with Mr. Dearinger. I, in fact, have been doing a great deal of thinking, reminiscing and soul searching. I can only guess what went wrong with our relationship. I cannot figure out why you did what you did. I look at our scrapbooks and see love. They contain thousands of evidential items that prove our wonderful time together as father and daughter. They have prompted me to write these letters and poems to you. I need you to realize how I feel, if not now, then later. Of course, I cannot write everything, but enough to express my side of the story. I need some measure of venting I guess. I cannot send them to you for I cannot have contact with you at this time. Mr. Dearinger told me that your mother was getting a restraining order so that I couldn't see you. I have heard nothing and seen no serving of a restraining order. This whole situation is quite perplexing to me and seems a bit complicated.

I hope someday you will look at your scrapbooks, read these letters and realize about what I am writing. I, however, have a feeling you have not forgotten our time together. I suspect you remember too well the reason you caused us to be estranged. I pray for you every day. .

Sincerely,

Dad

Dear Angela – *Ultrasound*

Let me start by describing what took place about fifteen weeks before you were born. I was at the hospital during your first ultrasound. The young woman who was operating the machine kept giving us partial descriptions of what she was seeing on the screen.

"Oh my," she exclaimed.

I asked what that meant and she exclaimed that there were two fetuses.

"Do you want to know the sex?"

We agreed to know. She said there were twin girls and asked if we wanted to see.

"Of course," we said.

I kept saying," Oh gees." I asked if she was sure. I could only see one at a time.

She said of course. "This is a new machine and I just trained on it. I know what I see for sure."

"Oh gees, oh gees," I kept saying.

It was overwhelming. I looked at you and Kaitlyn in all your glorious humanity. It was at that point that I dedicated the rest of my life to you two girls. I changed very much in a matter of minutes. I would never be the same. I later named you while your mother named Kaitlyn. Angela, you were my little angel.

I had originally dispelled and fought the idea of having more children, but later acquiesced to about ninety percent agreeable. I changed my mind during those first few ultrasound moments. I looked at both of you girls with a completely new attitude. I could see everything by means of the ultrasound. You were whole in every way. I could see your heads, torso, arms, legs and feet. You girls were indeed tiny little human beings. You were miracles for sure. I had seen an ultrasound before of Brook and Kristen, but not so clearly. I could nearly see your faces. I guess now days, even ultrasound faces are clear.

I silently introduced myself to you both that day. I became one hundred percent agreeable to having more children with the viewing of a few ounces of miracle essence. Humanity yet warms my heart. I see it everywhere. I see it clearly in you all the time.

I calculated how old I would be when you graduated from high school, then college. Sixty-nine seemed like a long time away. The years have flown. Life surely did not turn out the way I planned. It certainly has had highest highs and lowest lows. I do not have any regrets. I just wonder why God wanted me to experience you two girls, with all the joy and sorrow, with all the pleasure and pain.

"And what have I learned?" I ask. "What have I learned that I can share?"

I hope that there is some knowledge and wisdom buried in these letters. I hope that they are tiny bridges to the future. Optimistically, they will open the door to expanded spirituality for both of us and anyone else who decides to participate in my thinking, reminiscing and soul searching.

Sincerely,

Dad

Angels Sang

When God's
spirit pieces
intermingled,
angels sang
hallelujah and
holy, holy.
Two spiritual
beings to earth
plunged with
divine awareness.

Planets rotated while
measuring time.
Distant stars
confirmed celestial
paths.
Thunder roared and
lightening
momentarily flashed
inside two small
universe parts
seeking humanity.

Life
sparked and
created hope.
Hope quelled
fear and
potential
tragedy.
Glimmering
option seeds
continued future fire.

*Another good and
evil struggle
began in a
fragile moment.
Human nature
emerged while
wary angels
watched and
whispered
necessary words.*

Dear Angela – *Premature*

Your mother's pregnancy was normal until about thirty weeks of your life. A recent ultrasound indicated that everything was ok with your development, and that you were two weeks ahead of a single child because of being twins. Your mother's pregnancy then became a problem very fast. We saw our family doctor and he immediately sent us to Methodist Hospital at Indianapolis. The doctor at Crawfordsville didn't say much, but when we got to Methodist, everyone got excited after a couple of examinations. I think the condition is named *preeclampsia*.

Anyway, it meant that you two were ready to come out and it was not time. There were all kinds of complications. The last doctor we talked with put your mother in the pre-natal intensive care unit immediately. He confirmed the diagnosis of preeclampsia and said you girls were indeed insisting on coming out. He said that was unacceptable at thirty weeks. I think it was your idea to come out early because your umbilical cord was too small. Kaitlyn had a large cord, but yours was smaller than my little finger and you were starving. You had even lost weight during the last couple of weeks since the last ultrasound. You were very anxious, frantically swimming around inside your mother. She received enough treatment for the condition to settle everything down and convince you to wait for a couple of weeks.

They put monitors on your mother and I could listen to both of your heartbeats. I was sort of in touch with you even before birth. They finally gave your mother a new kind of medicine, in the form of a shot that was supposed to speed up lung development. We later found out that it worked. It was something innovative at the time.

I think they scraped your calf when giving that lung development shot. It was with a long scary needle. I don't know if your mother actually saw it or not. They inserted it through her belly button and into the embryonic fluid. The doctor scratched you with the needle while you swam around inside your mother. You wound up with a scar shaped like an "Ankh." You know that Egyptian Ankh Cross, known as the "key of life" or "eternal life." I don't remember if you yet have it on your calf. It might have faded with age.

We all waited during the two weeks while you nervously swam around most of the time while Kaitlyn casually sat down there at the opening waiting to come out. I don't know if your personalities were yet developed, but you were anxious and Kaitlyn laid-back. That seemed about right after you were born, you a little fearful, Kaitlyn daring. I think your personalities were forming at that time.

While closing in on the day of your possible birth, time became more a matter of you not wanting to wait longer and the doctors needing a few more days.

All of a sudden they took the monitors off. I missed being in contact with you, but evidently it was nearing time for your delivery. I missed being in contact with you girls. It was like being in the dark and I had to use my imagination. I was ready to spend some real time with you girls, but then they changed their minds and put everything back in a holding pattern for some reason unexplained to me. It was sort of a rollercoaster ride for everyone and especially for you I'm sure.

"We need just a few more days." The doctor said. "We would like to keep them in there until 32 weeks. That is when babies develop how to suckle."

The doctors kept working at keeping you in your mother's belly as long as they could. It was like a game, they wanting to keep you in there as long as possible, and you wanting to be born.

I had to go home to our retail store and take care of things in Crawfordsville. They said it would be awhile.

I got a call the next morning. A nurse told me that I should come over right away because it was about time for you girls to enter the world. I rushed around getting to the hospital. In fact, I rushed too much because the Crawfordsville police called me later asking where I was and if I knew my store was unlocked.

"I guess I was a little excited when I left, and no, I don't want my store unlocked," I uneasily told the police.

They said for me to relax about it and that they would lock the place. I remember rushing to Indianapolis in our Dodge Caravan. It didn't have much power, but I pushed it never the less. I was afraid of getting a ticket, but thought I had a good excuse if the police stopped me. I still don't know if that is a good excuse or not. I'm sure it's not, but anyway, I didn't get a ticket.

It wasn't long before you girls were ready to be born and I got there just in time to help, or pretend to help you, your sister and your mother.

You came out pretty fast after they said, "Let it happen."

I watched you being born. There were all kinds of people there, but I really only noticed you girls. I guess I had sympathy pains or something because my back was killing me. The nurse asked me if I was going to be all right.

"Of course, no problem," I answered, but I was not so sure. My back was killing me. There was just too much going on for me to worry about back pain.

Kaitlyn came into the world first and was so still that I was worried. You followed only a few minutes later. Both of you were very small and your little bodies looked extremely frail. Your skin had a gray tint at first, but soon got more flesh colored. Two nurses rushed Kaitlyn away. Soon you made a little sound that was not exactly a cry, but it was music to my ears to know you were indeed alive. I had just enough time to count your fingers and toes.

"Just the right amount of everything," I thought.

There were three doctors and several nurses in the delivery room. There was a delivery group and an intensive care group. I think overall, there were about eleven people in the delivery room. They took both of you immediately to intensive care. I got a quick glance before you were hurried off to the ICU. I had enough time to conclude that you both looked exactly alike. It was exciting.

I later saw you both in incubators and got to hold you about twelve hours later. You were both so tiny. I kept fighting back tears just looking at you. I went from one of you to the other, comparing every feature. You looked vaguely different, but when I looked at each feature, you were the same. Kaitlyn was slightly bigger. She weighed three pounds-seven ounces and you three pounds-two ounces. Five ounces doesn't seem like much, but when that small, it made a difference. I finally held you in my hands. Even though there was a difference in size, you both were very tiny and fit in one of my hands. Your head was about the size of a small apple. I could not take my eyes off your miniature features. I remember very well looking at those tiny, tiny fingernails. Wow, the beauty of life awed me.

Your small chest moved ever so slightly. I could only imagine your miniature heart beating. The whole life process was amazing. I couldn't help but constantly stare through the Plexiglas incubator, and then later when I held you in my hands. I could not help but tear up frequently. I felt as if angels were around, watching over us, reminding me how to love.

I was the first one to feed you. I think it was an ounce of liquid that the nurse handed me in a small vile. I gave the cream-colored liquid to you with something that looked like an eyedropper. It was very exciting and solemn to be with you in that holy place, that intensive care unit where you lived for a month, where angels silently watched over everyone.

Sincerely,

Dad

Holy, Holy, Holy

I touched
your sweet faces,
gathered
own courage and
accepted two other
lives in my life.
Grave was
my fear, then
cheerful became
my mantra, for
angels gathered
beside me, and
I found
undiscovered joy.
I touched
your white hands,
gathered
own soul and
put two other
blessings in my heart.
Courage
replaced fear, then
wisdom sought
my thoughts, for
I heard
angels speak
Holy, Holy, Holy.

Dear Angela – *Intensive Care*

We brought Kaitlyn home after two weeks, but you had to stay a month in the ICU. You both had to weigh four pounds before being allowed to leave the hospital. Of course, by you weighing only three pounds-two ounces, you had to gain more weight. It was difficult taking Kaitlyn home and leaving you behind. You later said that you saw us leave with her and were scared. We came back the next day, but I guess you didn't know where we went and had no concept of time.

I think that you might have seen us leave, but I also think that you couldn't have reasoned that we were leaving you behind. I believe that we register all seeing, feeling and learning from the first moment of our earthly life. Perhaps even in the womb, we record such experiences in our brain. We later put names, definitions and descriptions to that previously experienced, and then call it learning and remembering. I guess true learning is what we remember.

It was very difficult leaving you alone when taking Kaitlyn home. It was wonderful finally getting you home with Kaitlyn. Your mother's mother came up from Florida to help take care of you for a few months. You needed at lot of attention and she did a good job. She was with us for about three months.

I held you on my stomach a lot. I think you liked it there because I was always warm. You both liked it there, even when you got older. I have pictures of you girls on my chest. I loved having you there. We spent much time together after I took the teaching job and quit manufacturing. Your mother and I yet operated the retail store for a while longer. I remodeled an area in the store, constructing an office, kitchen and a living room in the back. There was already a bathroom there, so we were all set. You girls went to work with your mother. We had a woman come in to take care of you during the day there at the store. Everything seemed to work out pretty well. It was all of us together all of the time, including Freckles, the English Setter.

Freckles would sit in a street display window and invite people to enter the store. Many people stopped to admire her. She paid no attention to those who knocked on the window to get her attention. I witnessed many people coming in to pet her, and, of course, they then looked around once in the store. She was a good sales clerk, up to a point. She couldn't make the deal or close the sale, but she served as a good representative.

We finally closed the retail store and had a great going out of business sale. Seems everyone wants a good deal. I even brought in more metal combination couch and futon beds just so they could have that good deal. I marked them down, made a little money and everyone benefitted.

You girls and your mother stayed home after we went out of business. I think that was the best of times when we were all home and I only had to leave to teach. It was great to get down to one job. I had all that time to be with you girls.

Thinking about your early years brings back memories of my early years. I don't remember either of you having bad dreams in those early years. You later had bad dreams, or what might be called nightmares, but not when you and Kaitlyn had each other.

I remember when you visited during the summer and wanted me to stay with you until you went to sleep. You said you had bad dreams at home also. I would sit on the bedside or lay beside you after saying prayers. I often went to sleep myself. You hardly ever had nightmares, but were afraid you would have them. I remember a few times when you woke up scared, but couldn't tell me about what was scaring you. I think that lasted a couple of years. Kristen used to have bad dreams even as a young adult, but they always concerned a big knife. She laughs about it now, but certainly not then.

Some things never change. I think all kids have bad dreams at some time during their childhood. I wonder if you ever had such fantasies as I describe in the following poem. I guess I'll throw it in here. It rather describes the way I was when I was a small child and the way I am now as an adult.

Sincerely,

Dad

Bears Down Around

I wish to
live in
peaceful space,
passing time by a
comfortable
fireplace,
warming face,
soothing soul.

Yet,
I'm here in a
chilly bedroom,
storm brewing,
weather war
raging in
dawn's wary
tolerance.

I wish to
pull soft
down comforter
over head like
I used to do,
not letting bears
crawl down and
around my neck.

When I was
childish,
bears tried to
penetrate covers, but
now as a
candid adult,
they seem to
invade my mind.

When did I
grow up?
Why didn't I
remain
innocent, with
only silly bears to
attend to
nightly fears.

Storms now
creep near window,
threatening to
break it while
more than bears
sneak into
my reasoning
mind.

I wish I
could go back,
like my computer,
reboot and
reinstall
my system, and
restore
my C drive.

I wish I
could be
childish again
in my little
world room,
letting someone
else
be responsible.

Dear Angela – *Grandmother*

I know you will not remember my mother, your grandmother Louise. We were going to visit her during Christmas of 1993. It was your first Christmas. You girls were doing great, getting past nearly all signs of prematurity. We didn't make it to her house because of a heavy predicted snowstorm just before Christmas Day. We decided not to take a chance concerning driving problems, so we planned our visit sometime after Christmas. I yet regret not going because the weather cleared and the snow was not as heavy as predicted.

I say this because my mother passed about two weeks after Christmas. She had gone that day to get her hair done at the hair salon. She really liked going there and getting all fixed up pretty. A friend found her the next day in her bed, apparently having had a heart attack during the night. That person said she had a pleasant look on her face, but that was no consolation for her dying and us not seeing her before she died.

My mother was 79 years old and was yet cute. All the men liked her at the senior citizens' center. In addition, she could still bake a mean pie. Her chicken and noodles dish was also supreme. My other two kids used to ask for chicken and noodles every time we visited her. She was five feet tall, a little round and yet full of energy. She was a special person who had much love to share. I wish you could have known her. I remember when eleven years old walking down the sidewalk in Terre Haute, thinking that I was a big tall person, nearly a man in fact. I thought this because I was looking down at my mother. I didn't realize that she was only five feet tall. She never realized that fact either. I should have had a better perspective because my dad was six feet four. He towered over my mother and me. That day was different. I just felt tall and manly.

That reminds me of a time when I was about fifteen years old. I was a big kid by then, probably about six feet tall. For some reason I had problems with my little brother, Warren. You know how things can escalate as tempers flare and words get exchanged, well that was one of those days. My mother decided that I was to receive a spanking. She finally turned the spanking into a switching and I was to bring her the switch. She had never switched me before, but had threatened to do such a thing. She hardly ever followed through with punishment. She taught me the difference between discipline and punishment. I learned self discipline from my parents' tolerant disciplinary teaching.

I said, "I'm too big to spank." She insisted on switching me and told me again to get a switch. I pushed her mentally too far. "No, I'm too big to spank," I insisted.

She finally got so frustrated that she began to cry and throw driveway rocks at me. I felt horrible for making my mother cry, but I never said anything to her. She went into the house, crying and humiliated. I felt horrible. I felt like a piece of crap, but I didn't follow up on my feelings. I never apologized.

When my father came home, he talked with me. "I understand you're too big to spank," he said.

"Yes, I think so."

He paused a while and then spoke softly. My father was six feet four and weighed two-hundred and seventy pounds. He was a big man. He told me several times as a joke that his belly, which was a little big, was his chest that had fallen. When he got angry and resolute, he was right. His belly went back up to his chest that day. He came out of his slight slump and got taller as his chest and shoulders got bigger. He straightened and swelled, and got much bigger. He wore a size eighteen ring. He had huge hands.

He pointed a big index finger at me. "Then you're big enough for me to kick your ass," he softly said while looking into my eyes.

I paused a few seconds, looked at him and then spoke softly, "I guess I'm not too big to spank."

I apologized to my mother soon after that talk with my dad. Our talk included several paragraphs of advice in a few short sentences. I learned two lessons that day: 1. respect women and 2. don't intimidate people. I vowed not to intimidate anyone again. I also showed only love and respect for my mother for the rest of her life. I also reasoned to respect all women, all females. That certainly has and will always include you, Angela. I also learned that I was not as big as thought and would later find out that there are many tough guys out there in the real world. I think my dad was one of them, but he was tough in many more ways than physically tough. I learned a lot from my dad.

He was a man of few words and could convey whole paragraphs of advice with one short sentence. My mother could give long lectures with a sweet voice that was pleasant, but I really didn't listen well. Listening to my father was a different matter. I took note when he spoke. I wanted to be like my dad. He used to call me his shadow. I was proud to be his shadow. I have very fond memories concerning my parents. I lost my dad at 68 to cancer. I also wish you could have known him. I could go on and on about my parents and my childhood, but these letters are not about my childhood. They are about your childhood.

Sincerely,

Dad

Dear Angela – *Safe Place*

You sure didn't have any reason to be afraid when growing up with Kaitlyn. It seemed that you couldn't have a safer place to grow-up. Your lives were near perfect once you reached your real birth date. You both started crying, eating and behaving like natural newborn babies. Before that, you sounded and acted like preemies.

As they say, "Life is good."

That was a time before those two young men started the company; *Life is Good* and became millionaires. Debi gave me a hat and a shirt with that logo on them.

It's strange how life has its difficulties with no warning of intention. Just when we think everything is sunshine, gentle rain and rainbows, and the future looks bright, storm clouds appear and life turns to shit. Sorry about the language.

No one can predict the future and future planning seems futile, but we are too stupid to know it. We think we have some control. We can alter our short-term luck, but our long-term destiny is in other hands.

You and Kaitlyn had identical cribs and later shared a queen-size waterbed. You had identical clothes. You had identical hats to cover up your identical baldheads for nearly a year. You had identical shoes when starting to walk. Growing up beautifully was with both of you for sure.

Your bedroom gave warmth. Your night light gave security. Your parents gave plenty of love.

Seasons came and went, and you both grew like flowers in fertile soil. Life was good.

Sincerely,

Dad

Share a Ride

Destiny rides as if
on reluctant air
not knowing
highs and lows,
like someone seeking
only own path of
unimportance and
self triteness.

A safe place is a
sheltered place of
learning,
perceiving and
finding contentment.
It is like
rain growing flowers
in fertile fields and
loving insight
growing wisdom
in fertile minds.
It soothes souls.

Road forks are
decision places and
crux pauses of
destination throws, and
maps are for
journeys to new and
different places
conceived after arriving.

Dear Angela – *Distinguishing*

We bought a double side-by-side stroller, dressed you alike and everyone always asked how we identified each of you. It seemed not so difficult in person, but distinguishing in photos caused some problems for me. I yet today, have to study a picture to tell who is who.

You girls looked so much alike on the outside despite the differences on the inside. Kaitlyn was more outgoing and seemed more spontaneous. You were always cautious and a little anxious. I think that is from your early days in the womb where you were fighting for your life. You knew you had to get out of there one way or another. You just didn't know there was only one way out, and it had to be near the right time.

Twins are usually born a couple weeks early anyway, and a baby under stress a couple more weeks early. You and your mother were certainly under stress. Ok, that puts the calculated due date at thirty-six weeks. You girls were at thirty weeks when wishing to be born. That was not a good option. The doctors wanted to wait another two weeks. I think that was the longest two weeks of my life. I can imagine how long it must have been for you. Good thing you couldn't tell time and didn't have a calendar available. Maybe you did have a calendar in your brain and body.

The brain is yet growing, even though formed, at fifty-eight days in the womb. I believe that is when beginning awareness takes place, at or near that fifty-eighth day. I believe that is when the real you, when the heavenly spirit becomes aware of the earthly body. The real you is a spiritual being, placed there by God in your earthly body.

Therefore, I think you and Kaitlyn knew each other even before you were born. You could see, hear, feel and touch in the womb, and be aware of that limited world. I used to talk, sing and play the guitar for you when you were still in your mother's belly. I bet that was a nice place to be until you realized that you didn't have enough nutrients to remain healthy and alive. That had to be scary.

I think your basic personality was forming during that time. I believe that is why you are a little anxious and cautious even now. You will probably always be that way. It might be a good thing to be cautious, but not necessarily anxious.

I have said many times, "It is good to think too much rather than not enough."

Maybe you believe that also, but thinking must also follow truthfulness in order to foster correct reasoning and suitable action.

Sincerely,

Dad

Tear and Touch

There is a sterile
intensive place a
long distance from
where created;
where you gracefully fell,
becoming one with
prepared poise.
You waited sprouting;
then root, stem and
leaf grew with
resolved endurance.

You unfolded and
became beautiful,
red enough to
attract an eye and
delicate enough to
solicit a gentle touch.
You became tangible
in radiant sun
shining.
Wind caused
your beauty to
sway while
rain washed
your spirit clean.

Life seemed
simple on a
leisure stem where
you grew and
evolved.
Fast dancing
time embraced you.
It choked verve and

caused a beginning of
clumsiness.
You had only
time enough to
show gathered
splendor.

o

I heard a
shutter click,
motor rewind and
door open.

Then too soon,
you crumpled to
earth and
found organic
conclusion
like all
living entities.

I finally found
purpose in spirit,
through tears and
pain, and
now live your
beauty through
wall hanging as
framed digital bits,
enlarged enough to
attract tear and
touch.

You remain in
photo life,
even though,
no longer

in life form.
I can clearly yet
remember you
in real time, and
in split
moment still.

I now seek
your attention and
spiritual sharing as a
flower with a
short purpose for
my simple eyes and
complex mind.
I see you
in beautiful
photo rebirth.
I shall remain spiritually
in transition with you,
in digital display and
mental verve
until I also
again become a
seed dropped in a sterile
intensive place a
long distance from
where created.

o

I find true self
through thought,
meditation and
writing.
I resurrect history
through photography,
remembering and
mediation.

I realize fate
through listening,
praying and
following a
higher source.
I have but one
place to go,
pre-creation
anticipation place.

Dear Angela – *Attention*

Of course, you know that you were born March 29, but you don't know that soon after that day you girls were "up and at em," going places and getting much attention. A good example is by June, you were both ready and willing to greet the world. We took you to the Strawberry Festival on June 15 and you got a lot of attention. Aunt Venita and Uncle Stan were there with their stained and blasted glass. You girls got more attention than their artwork and I think Venita was a little jealous.

We had you in the side-by-side stroller and of course dressed alike. I think we liked the attention you got also. You girls were defining our lives even at that early age. You certainly were at the center of our lives. It was fun. We left you girls with someone else only one time. I guess you could say we only had one actual date after you were born. In retrospect, it was a mistake making you girls the whole of our lives, our life purpose, our destiny. There was always one of us with both of you all the time. I think you two were never separated. We went out on that date, just the two of us, but we didn't like it. We did the dinner, not the movie. We just wanted to return home to be with you girls.

For some reason I always thought someone was going to steal one of you, or both for that matter. It was a feeling I couldn't shake. We seldom spoke about it because it was scary, and besides, it seemed unreasonable and stupid. Maybe many parents feel that way, but my feelings were very strong and personal. Everything is personal when it is your own fears. A little fear is only little to someone else.

As John Mellencamp said, "There's no such thing as a small heart attack when it's you having it." I am probably paraphrasing rather than quoting, but you get the idea.

Little did we know that the fear was well grounded. We just didn't know who it would be or how it would happen. You girls were so beautiful, who wouldn't want to steal you?

We never left either one of you alone. We even got those human leashes that fastened around the waist when you were old enough to walk. We used them a few times when going to the mall or somewhere like that. We were thus attaching ourselves together all the time. You couldn't stray off or be snatched by someone. You girls could have the freedom of walking, but we could have the security of knowing you were close.

It seems somewhat silly now, but then we were serious. Fear was reading our intuitions correctly, but for the wrong reasons. Life lesson learning is best in retrospect. It's hard to read the tealeaves, hard to read the signs. It's hard to be a parent, hard to live with worrisome mind weights pressing down.

I used to say I wasn't afraid of anything except maybe a six foot eight man, weighing two-hundred-ninety pounds with a knife in his hand. I, however, found that philosophy not true.

I served in the Naval Security Group and might have met a few dangerous men. I might have participated in a few special tasks and seen some tough guys at work. I have been in some tight spots and done a few dangerous things.

Ok, that stuff scared me some, but my biggest fears are actually seen through a microscope and felt with a covert mind.

Sincerely,

Dad

Mind Weights

My fear weighs heavy
for those I love most.
Jeweled fears shake
my mental roof and
shatter my cranial walls.
It weighs me down with
"protect this" and
"protect that"
orders that freak me out.
I wear my armor far beyond
hills and crashing oceans.
I listen to oceans breaking and
mountains shuddering.
I think and pay attention, but
no solace comes to mind.
Fear is a state of mind and a
social point of view.
I cannot remove false trust and
shed mind weights.
For some reason I need
them for others' protection.
I wish my head to be
gleaming jewel-full and
my hands tranquilly
weight-empty.
I wish to trust myself, but
truth is burning and
hope is confusing.
On faith is about all
I can rely.

Dear Angela – *Freckles*

I'm sure you remember Freckles, the English Setter that we had when you were young. I'm sure you have plenty of pictures of her. She died when you were about four years old. She was a great dog and you girls played with her a lot. She had a perfect Zen disposition. I think we all learned much from her. In a strange way, you have some of her traits.

You seem to be tolerant and don't get too excited if things don't go your way. This sort of goes against the idea that you are a bit nervous and anxious about new things. Yet, when having time to study new things, you settle down into a Zen flow. You have had many disappointments over the years and I've always admired how you go with the flow and never let setbacks make you sad. At least, I hope they never make you sad, but then again, you don't show emotions very much.

Freckles was a great companion and I hope you remember her well. I only have a couple of pictures that I could show you. I have more memories than pictures. I also have mental movies that I can play of her in different settings and situations. I suspect your mother has several pictures of her. I remember one time we took her to Steve Swick's house where there was a large pond. There were two ducks on the pond and they swam out in front of her as she tried to catch up with them. They had no problem staying ahead of her. I think they were playing a game with her. She swam and swam, and got so tired that only her eyes and nose were showing above the water. She finally got so tired of swimming that she could barely make it to the shore. Once there, she couldn't pull herself out of the water. She was too weak to walk or even crawl out of the water. We had to lift her out and let her rest on the bank for some time. I think she would have gone back in the water if we had allowed it.

I remember another time when we first took her to the farm. She ran all over the forty acres for hours. She finally came back near us to rest, and then took off again right away. She ran all day in the woods. The next day she could barely walk because of being sore. It took her three days to limber up.

She used to look inside the refrigerator every time it was opened. She was too tired and sore to make it to the refrigerator after that day in the woods. I knew for sure she was hurting when that happened. We never gave her food from the refrigerator, but she always looked inside as if expecting some. I still don't know what her fascination was with it. I guess the odors were too compelling for her to resist. She did like to eat human food. She liked cleaning up under the table when you girls dropped food. She loved it.

She got over being sore in a few days and never exerted herself like that again. She learned to pace herself and somehow reasoned, if a dog can reason, that she would be returning to the farm and finally live there. I know, I know, dogs can't reason, but she was a very smart dog. She loved the farm with the pastures, creeks and woods. She was very happy there. You were also very happy there.

Freckles was my all time favorite dog. I helped her stay alive for a few days until your mother and you returned home from Mentor, Ohio. She got sick, mostly I think from old age and arthritis. She finally got so weak that she couldn't walk or even stand. She held out and was very brave during her last days. I will tell you more about that later if you are interested.

She was your mother's dog before I appeared on the scene. I learned to love that dog over the years. Like I said, she had a Zen personality, and I can appreciate that philosophy. Zen is a way of life that allows one to flow like a river, flowing with least resistance. I think you already know about Zen, even though never studying it.

I think that is why I like the river place so much. I can sit and watch the river flow for hours. Another thing I like about the river is that it constantly changes, sometimes hour by hour, for sure day by day. It changes with seasons, temperatures and amounts of rainfall. It is silently dynamic, making a statement by just flowing. It speaks to me.

They say the Wabash River was the largest river in the world during the Ice Age, when the glaciers were melting. You can see the original banks of the river. They are about eight miles apart there at Montezuma where the cabin is located. It was much wider farther south.

We are the same as a river, starting as a small drop of melted ice, growing into a stream, and then flowing like a river; except the river seems to have no ending time and we do. It seems to be forever to us, living our short lives, having our small purposes.

Sorry, I got off track. Freckles never had the chance to go to the river. I didn't own the river cabin during her lifetime, but I bet she would have loved it. I bet she would have loved swimming in that muddy river water. I'm not sure, however, that I would have wanted her to swim in the river. I often have the desire to swim in it myself, but I don't. I guess I will just continue to float up and down it in the boat, taking pictures and trying to catch fish. Catching fish, now that's another story. I won't go into the lack of catching fish right now, you know what I mean.

Sincerely,

Dad

Dear Angela – *Trees*

Aunt Venita gave each of you girls a tree for your first birthday. We planted them near the driveway, between the house and the barn. They were clearly in sight from the front and west side of the house.

I wonder if you remember much about that big white house and the horse barn. I totally remodeled that house, cleared the pasture of trash, small trees and old building materials. I built the garage, horse barn and a half mile of fence. I put a lot of love in that place. I always thought it would be the home place for you and Kaitlyn to come back to when grown.

You, however, left there when about five years old. We had a lot of fun there and built many memories in a short amount of time, at least many memories for me.

I remember much before I was two years old, but not many people do. I think it has to do with visual cognition or mental imaging in the brain. I bet Debi could tell us more about that type of learning and remembering.

I worked my ass off on that place, excuse the language, and gained a lot of satisfaction doing it. However, life takes its particular paths into the unknown. Life seems to not ask advice about how, why or where to go.

I was getting ready to say, "Life goes on," but it doesn't always go on. We painfully know that.

I hope you remember some things about that place. I can see it all in my mind, every wall, every door, every room. Matter of fact, I can play movies of it in my mind. I could draw you a picture of it. I could describe your room if you like. Maybe you remember it.

Anyway, I got off track. I was writing about Venita and the trees that she gave you girls. I don't remember what kind they were, but I do know they were alike and planted about eight feet apart. Your tree did very well, but Kaitlyn's tree died in less than a year. I didn't want to tell Venita that it died so I purchased another one just like it. I don't think Venita noticed that it was different when she visited. It looked nearly like the one she gave Kaitlyn. Well, that new one also died within a year. I never could figure out why because both of the trees were pretty much in the same place with the same soil and water.

I later took it as an ignored sign. I should have been more cognizant of what was happening. Your tree did fine and I bet it is big today. I will take that as a sign, even though you're not so healthy.

Venita also gave us a tree when Kaitlyn died. It was an evergreen tree called something like *Live Forever* or *Tree of Life* and it did live several years. I put it next to the deck at the big white house. I later planted it at Jenny's little farmhouse when I moved there. The deer ate it severely the first year. I moved it closer to the house and they also ate it the next year. It finally died.

There were just too many deer at Jenny's farm to grow a delicate tree like it. I also had to share my garden with deer, rabbits and who knows what other kind of animals. I finally accepted the idea of sharing my garden. So I planted more than I needed. I also planted many vegetables the animals didn't like to eat, but I didn't like them so much myself.

I used to see twenty or so deer come through the pasture. Sometimes I would see a bunch of them lying down in the backyard when I came home at night. They didn't even bother to get up when the headlights flashed on them. I guess they got very used to me. I bet you remember seeing them also.

Both of you girls got a cat. Yours lived, Kaitlyn's died. I will talk about that some later. Right now let me just say that there were many signs of tragedy coming and I never recognized them.

Ok, I got off track again. All I need to know these days, however, is that you are happy and alive. All I ever truly wanted and yet want is for you to be happy and alive. I will defer the healthiness some. I don't want to accept the truth that you have health problems, but I think we both have no choice. I sincerely wish I could take some of your hurt and pain. I wish you could let me know how you're doing. I want you to be that ever-living tree that lives a long, long time. I want you to be that planted tree at the big white house that yet lives. I need to go by that house some day and see how large it has become. I bet it has grown like you, tall and sturdy.

Sincerely,

Dad

Turning Cheek

I turn my cheek and
gaze afar while mind
threatens to splinter.
Like an oak roof beam
carrying a heavy load,
I cannot fatigue, sag or
crack from snowy days.

I philosophically
become a pine tree
showing a positive example.
I cannot follow oak ways,
cracking by not bending.
I must dry, age and season
to be truly useful.

I will mountain side live,
knowing no one can touch me
except changing winds.
No one can hurt me
when above yesterday's
consolation and
tomorrow's provocation.

Someday I will season well,
be good at turning cheek and
withstanding heavy loads.
I will bend without cracking
until honestly at life's end,
I will ash lie still while a
small oak box contains me.

Dear Angela – *Reluctant Cat*

Do you remember the little kitty cat we got from that young man down the road from us? I had him in school, but can only remember his last name, Barr. He lived near Emma. I don't think the cat wanted to come with us because it climbed up under the dash of our truck and hid until we carefully retrieved it. It later got under your waterbed and hid for a long time. We couldn't get to it without draining the waterbed. I emptied the bed of water and lifted the mattress while you grabbed the cat. It hid again for a long time. I don't remember where, but we didn't see it for a few days. I guess it got hungry or something and came out from the hiding place. We finally put it outside. It was happy there, but finally ran away or maybe a hawk ate it. I couldn't tell you the hawk possibility at the time.

I also had that big tomcat that came around and meowed for several days. I finally fed him. I knew that was a mistake because he made my place his new home. I didn't need a cat, but felt sorry for him. I had to admire his persistence.

The big tomcat liked my place until I went to Florida for a couple of weeks during Christmas. He was gone when I came back. I had left him plenty of food, water and shelter in the garage, but I guess that wasn't good enough for him. He came back a month later and tried to come inside, but I wouldn't let him in. I wanted him to be an outside cat. He left the next day. I think he went back to where someone allowed him inside, some place where it was warm. I didn't blame him at all. I only had him around to catch mice and I'm not sure he did a very good job at catching them anyway. I had plenty of mice around, especially during the fall season.

You remember, we didn't have good luck with cats. I never had one around long enough to get attached. That, however, changed when Debi and I adopted Kiddy Kidee. She has been a wonderful companion for all of us. I know you surely missed her when returning home from summer visits, but then again you had many animals down there in Georgia. We also had the horses, but you didn't ride them like your own.

Were you there when Dave, the ferrier, had that spiritual connection with Cherokee? I remember that we couldn't even trim his hooves. He would not stand still and one time even tried to hurt the ferrier that tried to trim his hooves. Dave kept talking to him and held the lead rope tight.

He kept saying, "Listen to me, listen to me," and Cherokee did finally listen.

He looked him in the eyes and spoke softly. Cherokee settled down and became a real gentleman after about twenty minutes. Dave kept saying repeatedly, "Listen to me, listen to me. Settle down, settle down."

I think something finally clicked in Cherokee's brain. He did listen and did settle down. Dave said, "This horse has been broken. He's not a wild horse. Someone has trained him and he has just forgotten. He just wants to do what he wants to do."

Dave went on to trim his hooves that day, and we even saddled and rode Cherokee some in the pasture. Dave said he was going to quit trimming hooves to become a part-time youth minister at his church and that we would have to find someone else the next time. We later retained the same ferrier as used before. I think he came to trim Cherokee's hooves with trepidation. He changed his mind after only a few minutes.

He said, "You've really been working with this horse, haven't you?"

I said, "A little bit."

"Well, this isn't the same horse. Are you sure you didn't switch horses on me?"

I then kept quiet. I shouldn't have taken the credit, but didn't know how to explain what had happened between Cherokee and Dave. I really didn't know what happened. How could I explain it? It was a spiritual thing.

Cherokee was a perfect gentleman. He stood still and even picked a hoof up for trimming. I couldn't believe what had happened between the horse and Dave and it continued with another ferrier. It was truly spiritual. I became a believer that the Holy Spirit is in all things and can flow like wind, water and gravity. There is no limit to the power of God. I couldn't believe that Cherokee's good behavior continued with you, me and the ferrier.

Oh, I also have to mention Buddy, the big brown dog, when talking about animals. He was awesome. He loved to catch ground hogs. He worked for a week or so down at Closers' farm and finally got a big groundhog. He came out of the ordeal with only a scratched nose, but then who knows what other injuries he suffered in the process of getting that thing. He got all dusty and dirty every day for a week. He then didn't go back, so I knew he was successful.

You have had many animals already in your life and you will have many more. They come in and out of our lives, living shortly, but appreciated while here. You're very good with animals for sure. It seems all animals like you. I always thought you would make a great veterinarian.

Sincerely,

Dad

CHAPTER II

Self Discovering

Dear Angela – *Personalities*

I remodeled the 3200 square foot farmhouse completely. It was a total mess when I bought it. It had only one room finished with drywall. Every other part of the house was bare studs and twenty year old exposed insulation. It had a working fireplace for heat and one partially finished bathroom. I did everything: electrical, plumbing, tile work, wall construction and drywall. I installed all the sinks and cabinets. It had twenty-year-old Celotex on the outside of the house, but no siding. I installed most of the siding, flashing and soffit.

The house did have, however, that beautiful front porch that stood twenty-two feet tall with four fourteen-inch square wooden pillars. That was the completed part of the house, except the porch roof leaked and the wooden ceiling was rotting. The house was striking, sitting on a gradually rising hill overlooking a circular driveway. There were trees and a partial stone fence out front, and on part of that stone fence was the name of the place, *Spring Falls*. Someone attached the metal name on top of the stone fence near the road long before I came long. Do you remember the name?

I also built a huge deck, garage and of course the horse barn. Ok, I got off the subject. Let me just say that I did everything except the heating and air conditioning and the carpet. I better quit bragging. I do have to admit that I was very proud of all the work put into that place. Did I mention all the woodwork and doors? Ok, enough, you say.

Your bedroom was upstairs on the southwest side of the house. There was also a guest bedroom on the other side of a large bathroom. On the front side of the upper level was the master suite that included a huge bathroom. It was a bedroom that I converted into a bathroom. Do you remember that huge bathtub in which you girls loved to play? The master suite had big closets and plenty of windows that overlooked the front lawn. Your room had two windows that overlooked the barn and pasture. You could see the horses from your windows.

You girls first had identical cribs, but it wasn't long before you shared a queen size waterbed. You loved that waterbed because it was always warm and comfortable. I liked to sometimes lay with you girls and take a short nap on that bed. It was the same waterbed from which we had to later extract the cat.

Those were great days. We read a book almost every night and when it was time to go to sleep, I said goodnight in a wonderful way. We said prayers and then I would kiss each of you girls goodnight. You only required one kiss and a little hug, but Kaitlyn required four kisses. One on the forehead, one on the chin and one on each cheek delivered in the motion of a cross. That was a wonderful ritual and I think you both got exactly the attention required.

I think Kaitlyn always required more attention than you did. She was outgoing and you were a little quiet. You both had great personalities that were different from each other. You both appeared slightly different, but when looking at separate features, I couldn't see any difference except for that little blue blood vein on your forehead. It was at the top of your nose. I don't remember when it disappeared or at least faded greatly.

Kaitlyn always weighed a few ounces more, but you were certainly identical in looks. You had many differences. I remember when you both got a taste of chocolate. I think you were about one and half years old. You were indifferent about it, but Kaitlyn loved it. Her eyes lit up and she certainly asked for more. I think even today, you don't like sweets all that much. Is that right? There were differences like that surfacing all the time. Who could predict where all that personality difference would lead? I wish she was yet here so we could see and learn many of the differences.

I think Kaitlyn was an extrovert and you, an introvert. I think you, however, over the years have changed. You have always been a bit bashful and reserved. You have always been reluctant to try new things, but get brave after once forcing yourself to try them. I remember several times like that when you were reluctant, but overcame your fear.

Remember the first time we went canoeing and you were afraid to get in the unstable canoe when it was even half on the bank? You were scared when we first hit a rock, but by the time we hit a few rocks and paddled down the creek a mile or so, you were looking for rocks to hit with the canoe. You got very brave. I had to say no to the rocks because I didn't want to damage the canoe. I think you were a little bit like that about horses at first, but it didn't take long before you were brave.

You are brave now, jumping and riding like a crazy woman. That jumping is scary to me. I have enjoyed watching you grow while learning to ride and jump the horses. I am always amazed how much you know about horses and horse care. I am truly surprised that you're not going into some kind of horse thing as a vocation.

Sincerely,

Dad

Cross Kisses

I touched her face with
four kisses placed
like a cross at night:
forehead, chin, cheek, cheek.
It was her way of
saying good-night and
I gratefully did it with
unconditional love.
I kissed her face and
felt her soul.
She a lady at three made
me a young man at fifty:
forehead, chin, cheek, cheek.
She was a
twin daughter
who gave short-lived life
new meaning.
Her sister required
only one kiss, but
I cherished her
with same grace.
Their love kept me
awake at night:
forehead, chin, cheek, cheek.
Those memories,
after all these years,
yet keep me
awake even though
they're gone,
one in heaven at
three and a half and
one five hundred miles
away at seventeen:

forehead, chin, cheek, cheek.
I count blessings
every morning, but
don't cross kiss at
night any more.

Dear Angela – *Signs*

I remember the two cats that we got as kittens for you girls when you were about two years old. You both immediately picked out the one you wanted and we brought them home that day. I can't remember what color they were exactly or their names, but I think yours was a light multicolor and Kaitlyn's was a dark multicolor. I think they were about a year old when Kaitlyn's cat found a hiding place under the deck and died. I couldn't retrieve it from under the far edge of the deck, and I remember it made a bad odor for several days.

Maybe I should have taken that as another sign to be more vigilant and protective, but I made nothing of it at the time. I never figured out what caused the cat's death. It never appeared to be sick and nothing could have killed it under the deck. Many thoughts haunt me. I fear that I did not take notice of enough signs. I have certainly gained respect for signs over the last few years.

I believe the spiritual world is as close as the end of my nose and I need to pay more attention to it. I think the Holy Spirit is very active in our lives. We need to listen and look more, actually hear and see more. There are signs all about us. We can discover that which is about and within us by opening mind and heart. After all, we are spiritual beings and the Holy Spirit lives within us if we believe in Christ. He is our connection to heaven, to eternal knowledge, to God. Oh, I wish I could be more aware of the spiritual world.

I also believe that the Holy Spirit is helping me write these letters to you, Angela. I hope I am doing a good job, for in my heart I feel, but seldom does my writing convey well enough, my true feelings. I have this problem all the time, even with the poetry, but writing about life with you and Kaitlyn is very difficult.

Do you ever feel Kaitlyn's presence? I used to more than I do now. I still feel that she visits occasionally. I still rub the oak box that contains her cremated ashes and think about her strongly. I don't receive any contact for which I wish while rubbing the oak ash box. You know though, at the oddest of times, I feel her presence. She visits on her own time schedule, not mine. It's like a brush of my cheek when lying in bed trying to sleep or like when I experience a butterfly seemingly wanting to land on my shoulder. Oh, I almost feel her presence now.

I get tears when I open my heart, mind and soul to her. I get tears sometimes when I think about you.

I hope you don't think that I'm strange. I hope whoever reads this book doesn't think that I'm strange. I think I'll just sit here quietly for a while.

Sincerely,

Dad

Stray Cats

Anxious stray cats
insecurely wander
my dark
alley mind
like wind blowing
through narrow
passageways.
They run past
mindful doors with
light hinges, and
through thin
non-insulated
hastily constructed
membrane walls.

Who creates
complex minds?
Who invites
dangerous cats?
Who allows
insecurity to exist?
Ravenous cats
seize and
threaten
my insecure space, a
born innocent
place where
clear mind
grows defectively.

I am an
insecure author of
precious memories
put into words,
written on cheap
paper with a
twenty-nine cent
ballpoint pen.

My stray animals
willfully write
shadowy poems
every night as if
they own
my mind or
rent enough
space to claim a
clear title.

How hungry are
those cats?
How narrow are
those paths?
How strong are
those winds?

Time will surely
tell if
protection fails,
doors open,
walls crumble and
cats scratch
their way through
delicate alley
archives.

Dare I sleep
tonight?
Dare I dream
tonight?
Dare I remember
wonderful days gone
like a bedroom, a
tree, a
daughter?

Dear Angela – *Picking Dandelions*

When you were about two years old and beginning to walk very fast, I lost sight of both of you. We were in the front yard where walnut trees and a few bushes grew, scattered here and there over about a half acre. I was picking up walnuts while you girls strolled around through and among the trees. All of a sudden, I didn't see either of you. I looked around the front lawn and not a glimpse. I walked a little faster while searching. Nothing, no sign of either of you. I started running about, while getting a little exited. I ran around the house to where the basement spring drained outside and created a swamp. We called it the bog. I was coming close to near panic.

I don't know if you remember that spring that fed a caldron in the basement. It constantly drained out near the north side of the house, keeping a constant water level in the caldron and a few inches of water in the bog outside. That bog contained a lot of soft black mud, tall grass and who knows what kind of hidden life. It was a cool sort of ecological system, but also a soft muddy quagmire. I feared you might have gone into that bog. I had no idea what might happen if a person did step into it, much less a little person. I ran to the bog and found no one. I ran around the house farther until I reached my starting point.

I panicked, running through the front lawn again, then around the house again. I finally ran near the road, and as I got near the road edge, I looked back and saw both of you standing near a big lilac bush. It had blocked my view. You were picking dandelions for a bouquet. Neither of you realized that I had been frightfully searching. I don't know why you didn't answer my calls or walk into my line of sight. All I knew was that I could only thank God for keeping you safe. The whole incident took probably two minutes, but it was a long anxious two minutes. You girls were never in danger. Only I was anxious and fearful. Only I needed spiritual comforting and some big hugs.

I remember losing Brook one time in the Thrifty Hardware store for about a minute. The front door, that was open for ventilation, was near a busy street. I had a minute of panic when he wandered away from me. I yet remember not knowing where he was for that little while. He was one aisle over, but it might as well have been ten thousand miles over. You girls might as well have been ten thousand miles away in my mind and heart. It's strange how a mind can play tricks on itself. It's strange how God teaches a lesson in a minute or two.

Sincerely,

Dad

Weight Lifter

My inhibited emotions are
sometimes like iron weights,
pulling me downward as if
hundred pound dumbbells
waging war against gravity and
I'm middle caught.

I wish to be where
colorful kites and
balloons float nearly
weightless in air.
I pray I shall not
fall into panic,
like in an ocean without a
life jacket, for surely
I will drown.

Seldom do my emotions
cause anxiety, gush and
lash-out with fearful panic.
Oh, to be a carefree guy,
composed and smooth,
without lifter's burdens,
sitting in a quiet yard with
two little daughters,
seeking not world weight.

Dear Angela – *Riding Horses*

Do you remember how we used to go riding through Jenny Hays' two hundred acre woods? We started taking you with us when you were about four months old. I usually took Kaitlyn and your mother took you because Kaitlyn weighed a little bit more. The extra weight, only a few ounces and later several ounces, seemed to make a difference during the long ride. You girls would sit in the saddle on a small pillow in front of us and by the time we got back to the far end of the woods, you would both be asleep. The constant rocking and smooth rhythm was apparently a wonderful sensation.

Your small amount of weight seemed heavy by the time we returned. Holding your slumping body with one hand and the reins with the other hand proved to be a heavy load after a couple hours or so. I think it was about a six mile round trip. That was a long time when considering the horses only walked. I also remember your cat sometimes going with us. She pretended to be a dog, running alongside. The only thing was, the cat had short legs and couldn't run like a dog. The cat would peter-out and fall behind on the way back. Well, compare the length of horse legs and cat legs or even dog legs. I rest my defense of cat stamina.

Did you ever know that Jenny misnamed Dodger and Gartez? She switched their names by mistake, telling us wrongly. By the time we found out that we were calling them the wrong names, they were just naturally Dodger and Gartez. It didn't really matter much because they seemed to fit their new names better. In the end, it really didn't matter because we called Gartez the name, Momma. We finally had to put Dodger down because he had arthritis so badly that he couldn't stand. He lay in the pasture for a day or so before I called the vet. He made a large round circle in the grass, moving around trying to get on his feet. I surmised that he would never stand again.

I tried to spare you from seeing the euthanasia process, but the woman I was dating at the time brought you home earlier than planned. You came out and saw him after the veterinarian had put him to sleep. You seemed to handle it very well, but then I always suspected that you knew more about life and death than I did. I remember when the vet injected that second syringe and the final vibration of Dodger left. I felt it leave. I didn't realize that he had a vibration until it was gone. Total death stillness is a spiritual thing.

Paul Dixon came with his backhoe and we buried him in the pasture beneath that big maple tree. He liked standing under it during hot summer days. That was where he laid down and never got up. You seemed to understand everything. I have learned more about life and death myself since that day, as time passes and God educates.

Momma died after I moved from Rock River Farm. We saw her once I think before she passed and she didn't look good at that time.

Do you remember the time when she laid down in the snow and having arthritis, couldn't get up? I finally got her up and into the barn, called the vet and he came and helped her. He gave her a shot and I kept her in the warm barn for several days. The vet said she suffered from hyperthermia. She finally got well. We nearly lost her that winter. She seemed to do just fine several following winters. I guess she learned to take better care of herself and especially to not lay in the snow on a severely cold winter day.

Sincerely,

Dad

She is Your Hope

Recovery speaks a
language seldom heard.
She is usually silent,
coaxing repel of
death and destruction.
Insurance is no answer,
yet it makes a mind ease.

Speak mind for
who else
knows it?
Control self for
who else can
understand it?

Last listen to Recovery,
call her name and
understand what she says.
She is your hope and faith.
She is your earthly way.
She is a soft spoken servant
you cannot ignore.

Speak mind for
who else
knows it?
Control self for
who else can
understand it?

Dear Angela – *Leg Messages*

I used to give you and Kaitlyn arm and leg massages, and when you were about two years old, I discovered some small bumps on your legs. We later found out that they were osteo condromas. I'm probably not spelling the words correctly, but anyway, they were small accumulating calcium deposits due to small cracks in your bones. They keep building calcium as if continually trying to repair the crack. They are similar to a little raised place where a bone was broken and repaired. These little raised bumps, however, keep growing and building until noticeable, and then become larger and problematic. Some of them are not noticeable. Some of them are deep beneath the body's surface. I know they are yet a big problem today for you. You told me once that you have hundreds of them. You have had some operations to remove them where they caused problems of pain and motion. I deeply feel for you. I wish I could do something about them. I hope someone can someday do more about them than they can now.

The doctor was surprised that I found them at such an early age. It was due to those massages that you liked so much. They are a little bit unusual, but not unique to your situation. Kaitlyn had to have one of them removed at Riley Hospital when she was less than three years old. They sized her for a cast before operating. She later had to have a brace that helped support the leg. It seemed to work pretty well and she walked correctly again in no time at all. I think the condroma was pressing against a nerve and that was a real problem. She was dragging her leg. It became noticeable quickly. One of your operations was similar. You also had a brace after your operation, but your leg never came back to full use. I wish I knew more about your health. I wish you were yet communicating with me. You never did tell me much about your health or even your education as a matter of fact.

I never got medical or educational information at all after you moved to Florida. I sure missed a lot by not being around you every week.

I don't want to go into that right now, but just let me say that I was saddened a lot by not being around you often, and being unable to help and comfort you. I yet feel that way.

Sincerely,

Dad

Tired Eyes

My thoughts accumulate
like images on silver painted glass,
not a window, but a mirror
existing so that I might learn
about genuine self.

I have no answers, but only
questions to be answered.
I can't hear a sea melody
coming across water like
good sense and security.
I don't know where sea
foam goes when waves
resend energy to undertow,
to some invisible power
taking life away beneath
my brief observation.

An ocean breaks and
breaks until tired eyes
fail to see reality.
A person takes and
takes until a mind can't
remember illusion well.
A curved horizon bends
without skill or reservation.
It blindly hides until
ocean is nonexistent.
I ask how can something
vanish before eyes while
intently watching.
Blackness has no equal.

My words liquefy into
thoughts and flow like tears,
wishing not to become waves,
become horizon like,
vanishing with undertow,
beneath crashing intentions.
I can only lay back and
enjoy inner gaze where silver and
glass are associates, and
reflection shapes
my remembering, but
fading, mind.

Dear Angela – *Clown*

I have this picture of us when we were in the Riley Hospital waiting room just before Kaitlyn's fitting for the leg cast. We were all sitting on a bench while someone took a picture of us with our camera.

The interesting thing about the picture, when we got it developed, was that a person dressed as a clown was standing behind Kaitlyn. The person had a white face from what appeared to be a lot of make-up. I thought it was somewhat weird at the time because I didn't remember a clown being behind us. No one remembered a clown being behind us during the picture taking. No one remembered a clown being at the hospital that day.

The person appeared be a clown, but in retrospect I'm not so sure it was a clown. I didn't question anything at the time. We were preoccupied concerning Kaitlyn's surgery. I later thought the clown looked more like a spirit or a spiritual being. I worked hard to get that photo from your mother because it meant a lot to me. I now definitely see the clown as a spirit, another sign, another omen that I ignored. I have become much more spiritual since seeing that clown. I'm not sure where that photo is now. I will look for it very soon and make sure I have it. It seems hard for me to keep track of that picture. I hope I haven't lost it. I think I put it in a safe place and now can't remember the safe place. It's strange how I can remember so many details of our history, but can't keep track of that photo. I hope you read these letters some day with enjoyment and look at that picture.

Sincerely,

Dad

Dear Angela – *We Were Blessed*

I think back about those days at Riley Hospital when both of you girls were healthy. The condromas were puzzling for sure, but the doctor seemed to think they wouldn't be a big problem. You girls would have several of them and if they didn't get into your joints, they would not be too serious. The doctor also said that by the time they caused arthritis, medicine would be available to combat the caused problems. He thought that maybe arthritis would be a problem when you were fifty or sixty years old.

Well, I guess he was wrong because you already have arthritis and it is a problem. Anyway, at that time we were yet feeling blessed for sure. You girls were beautiful and healthy.

Kaitlyn did develop that one problematic condroma on her leg. Apparently, one of those calcium deposits was pressing on a nerve in her leg. Yours was the same I think, but on the opposite leg. They both were right below the knee on the outside the leg.

Kaitlyn's operation was successful and the final solving of the problem was the cast for rehabilitation purposes. I was impressed with the doctor. I wish I could remember his name. I understood that everyone respected him in the field of orthopedics. I later found out that he contracted some disease where he lost much use of his hands. Imagine that, a surgeon who developed some muscular disease in his hands. God sure has an odd way of using people.

As it turned out, the doctor said, "I can only operate on a few people a day, but can train many to operate through my instruction."

He thought the disease was a blessing. That was a wonderful spiritual way of looking at things.

Kaitlyn had to wear a brace for quite a while, but her leg recovered just fine. We first noticed that she was dragging her leg slightly. It got worse until she couldn't walk very well, but after the operation, she walked fine after a few months.

You had a similar operation a few years later. You now have had other operations on your leg, shoulder and elbow. I certainly sympathized with Kaitlyn and now sympathize with you for having to cope with those damn osteo condromas. Little did I know it was just the beginning of your problems. I wish I could have helped more, then and now. I was able to show some concern then, but now we are drifting apart. It, however, doesn't keep me from feeling the way I do. I love you so much.

Sincerely,

Dad

Dear Angela – *Home Place*

Do you remember when I built the horse barn and the white painted board fence? I surely worked hard on that building and built all the stalls out of rough sawed oak purchased directly from the sawmill. I air-dried the lumber in the garage for a year before using it on the barn and fence. I doubt if you remember the finished tack room with drywall, trim and baseboard. I made special racks for the saddles and hangers for the halters and bridles. I have to admit that it was very nice.

I especially worked hard digging all those postholes by hand. I cut all the post tops at an angle and the poplar wood fence boards at the correct length. I finally got someone to come and drive the last posts in the woods area. He had a machine that drove the post into the ground and through the roots. That was a great help. I would never have gotten those postholes dug because of all the tree roots.

Anyway, we had a good time out there in the barn and pasture with the horses. We rode horses and riding lawn mowers out in the pasture. I was always working on that place as if thinking it was going to be some kind of legacy place where you girls would have growing-up memories and come back to visit.

It was a beautiful place, with the big-pillared white house, white garage, white barn and white fence. I always wanted one of those places that everyone in the family called the "home place." I put a lot of love into that place. Life was good there at Spring Falls.

You know though, time has taught me that there aren't very many home places. For example, the farmhouse and buildings where I grew up are completely gone now. They tore the house down first, and then a couple of barns and finally everything man-made was gone. Only trees, grass, memories and a few foundation remnants are now present, and of course the beautiful farm land. Those few signs of where buildings once stood are about all that is left of man's influence, of our family influence. I once walked Debi through my old house from remaining foundation remnants.

"Here was the kitchen. Here was where I watched TV. Here was the front porch where my dad and I watched thunderstorms," I pointed out while speaking.

She had to imagine everything. I saw it all clearly in my mind, playing articulate movies of my past, as if being there only yesterday.

"Here was where we played canasta. Here was where I pretended to do math which was the only book I brought home to study."

I made good grades without homework. I actually seldom studied that math book. I just brought it home with good intentions. I always had a study hall where I did my homework. I guess we had less homework in those days. You know though, I think the standards were higher back then. I think we just didn't study as many subjects. We studied basics. I'm a basics kind of guy anyway. That was handy in those days and even today I think. Yes, my old home place is all down to memories and words. My parents are also down to memories and words. So "home places" seldom exist, and if they do, not for long.

I don't need a home place now. Your mother and I didn't have a typical marriage, but I thought we were happy. I guess there was too much difference in our ages, too much difference in our personalities or just too much difference in general. I, however, thought she had what she wanted and I surely had what I thought I wanted.

I remember working for two straight years without taking one day off while remodeling that big white house, the so called would be home place. I was working on the house and manufacturing waterbed drawer pedestals at the same time. I also had some rental houses at the time and helped your mother with the retail store. I was a busy man, but that was all before you girls came along. Things changed after you girls arrived.

Sincerely,

Dad

Un-mended

I stare at my
clasped hands,
battered flesh,
callused palms,
torn finger nails.
Prayer is in them.
Some would say,
I need a
manicure badly;
never had one,
never will I suspect.

Who will ask for one
up there at that
fancy place,
skyward located?
Will I have to
dress up and
get cleaned up for
special occasions?
Who will
introduce me
in heaven?

I work days
making furniture and
sleep nights
mending body.
Prayer is in
more than my hands.
Life wears me down.
Ending last days,
worn-out and
un-mended,
would be heaven.

Prayer is in my soul.
Perhaps I won't
need a manicure when
seeking a final
resting place.
Surely my rough exterior
will be overlooked
in heaven and
my soft
gentle nature
will be appreciated.

Several More Years

I finally found that
place to belong and
it was within myself
while passing through a
creating universe.

I now sparingly and
uniquely share that
place in quiet
mental repose with
discovery in my soul

I am taking a well
deserved rest as
might an old man do
when life presses not and
death is bearing down.

I am in age denial.
I don't see or
hear reminders, and
in this state of affairs,
I think I shall live forever.

Familiar Way

I am water
flowing over
smooth rocks.
Objects placed
before me in
sparkling light's
warm array
guide me
towards a sea.
Each rain drop
collected by
each dancing ripple
expands and
becomes
more than self.
Each stream,
each river
becomes
more than self.
And into that
sea I plunge to
become
mighty and
able to carry a
world towards
tomorrow.

CHAPTER III

Soul Collecting

Dear Angela – *Teaching*

Things got a bit financially tougher when you girls were born, however, I got my old teaching job back just in time to get good insurance and a steady paycheck. The Good Lord was looking over us. I did all right in the teaching deal because Gary Wineger had a stroke about the sixth week of the new school year. He was the other part of the teaching deal. It didn't seem quite fair for him.

It was the first year in the new high school building. Chuck Fiedler asked me to substitute for Gary until he got better from his stroke.

"If he doesn't get better, think about staying on," Chuck said.

I had quit teaching because I burned out on those middle school kids, so I wasn't sure if I would want to stay on or not. I took the temporary substituting job and Gary didn't get any better. Chuck asked me to stay on after the first semester and to that I agreed.

That was a lesson in itself when he asked me back into the school system. I had burned out at the middle school and was looking for an excuse to leave, and finally did leave after I met your mother. Moving to Florida seemed a perfect thing to do and I thought I had gained a new friend. Even though I was burning out, I worked hard and did a good job until the last day. Therefore, when it came time to be re-hired, Chuck knew that I was a good man and had worked hard up until the last day while previously employed in the school system. We were also good friends and that didn't hurt any either. He had confidence that I would do a good job. Therefore, Chuck Fiedler was the one responsible for getting me back into teaching. I owe Chuck a lot for helping me out when I needed help.

The teaching situation left a bittersweet taste in my mouth about Gary. I felt bad that he had the stroke, but I was also somewhat glad he did because that opened the door for me. It just didn't seem right to be happy about someone having a stroke, but that was life, bittersweet life. The only solace was that Gary was just a year from retirement and that the job would have opened up soon anyway. I don't think I could have waited two years on Gary, but one, yes.

I needed a steady paycheck and a good insurance plan. I needed better insurance for sure, and later I really needed better insurance. I needed good insurance when you girls were born, but didn't have it. I think the hospital bill was around sixty-eight thousand dollars. I had to sell a house to pay for our part of the bill. It was not a big house, and not totally paid for, but it needed selling. I think we needed about twelve thousand dollars for our part of the hospital bill. At least I had the house to sell, right? I certainly didn't mind selling it, that's for sure. I was more than glad to give you girls anything and everything I had if necessary. Oh, what a dynamic time it was in those early days.

Ok, let me get back on track concerning the teaching. Crawfordsville High School moved into the new school building that year and had older students than I previously taught. I realized during that first returning semester that I was yet a natural born teacher. I also appreciated the fact that I picked-up where I left off and got a nice raise while not teaching. Teachers had received several raises while I was gone. I also got full credit for my teaching years. The subject matter turned out needing a complete updating. I got into computers, robotics, CNC machines and automation. As it turned out those subjects sort of saved my enthusiasm for teaching later. A man named Kris Rowland who worked at California Pellet Mill Company really helped me along those lines. He was like an angel that came along just when I needed one. I'll talk about him later.

Things were really looking up. I had the house all remodeled, a job I liked with benefits and my family about me. Life was good.

Sincerely,

Dad

Sweet Life

Echoes and sunlight
crowd my mind.
I can't see
tomorrow for today.
I am blind with
ideas and
deaf to suggestions.

Fascination begs like an
empty candy sack that
will not fill while
blindness and
deafness are seemingly
attributes of a man
who thinks too much.

Big plans wait on a
drawing board
next to a computer
placed on a desk
full of money.
I am blind with ideas and
deaf to suggestions.

Somehow, someway,
somewhere, sometime,
I futilely lost
my sense of taste.
My plans are ugly and
life isn't near
sweet anymore.

Dear Angela – *Patience*

Your mother taught me patience, my students taught me patience, but God taught me the best and most patience. I think once a person gets past the idea that love is the greatest thing one can give and receive, then humility and patience become very important. I have received lessons in patience all my life and have been trying to teach patience all my life, whether to children, students or employees.

Developing one's self is important. Freedom and acceptance of responsibility are great tools for fulfillment, but they require patience and self-control. I think humility is also key for success, but patience is the spiritual glue that holds personal life fulfillment together.

I believe that you, Angela, have taught me much about patience. I have watched you work with your horses, learn about taking care of them and loving them. I have seen you deal with life loss, divorce, disappointment, moving, new schools and new friends. I have seen you serve as a mediator between your mother and myself. I have seen you deal with more hardships than most people experience in a lifetime. My heart reaches out to you. I wish you could or would reach back to me.

Sincerely,

Dad

An Idea is Born

A brain is a
tricky thing as
it unconsciously
performs
mundane tasks
without effort or
awareness.

It allows life and
death to seek
destiny with a
little bit of
electricity and a
lot of
cell wiring.

It accepts
weightless
energy through
silent matter and
flowing blood, and
with light speed,
reveals mind.

A mind enters
exploitation where
dreams reside,
fantasy blooms and
no one but God
knows silent truth as
humanity seeks itself.

An idea is born
in some wonderful
deep personal place or

*from some external
alien space where
minds open and
thoughts swell.*

*Ideas are born
from thought seeds
planted,
germinated and
grown into
thoughts, words and
deeds.*

*Oh how
wonderful that
bundle of
soft tissue is
when mind seeks
shared expression
through awareness..*

*Oh how
wonderful that
emerging day is
when
fertilized ideas
become
mindful fruit.*

*Thoughts are born
painlessly silent with
little provocation, yet
inflame abundant
stars into
gloriously loud
universal notice.*

*How can something
so plentiful
be so valuable, as
unending thoughts
incubate ideas and
solutions
measure time?*

*We are bits of an
emerging universe of
weightless thought in
time and space,
giving birth to
magnificent
enduring humanity.*

Dear Angela – *A Spanking*

You and Kaitlyn were so easy to get along with and teach right from wrong. However, I remember one time when we were at church, sitting where the choir usually sits. I think it was a special service when needing more space. We were sitting near the emergency outside door. You girls seldom misbehaved, but that day you were giggling and talking during the service. I asked you to be quiet. I asked a couple of times and you didn't change your behavior. It was unusual for you to ignore the rules and thus I reacted accordingly. I finally warned you that I might have to give you both a spanking when we got home if you didn't straighten up.

You asked me, "What is a spanking?"

I said that I would demonstrate what it was when we got home. I did gently demonstrate on Kaitlyn when we got home. That was the only time I ever came close to spanking either of you or doing anything resembling physical discipline. It was a teaching moment I guess. I gently demonstrated with gentle pats. I put Kaitlyn over my knee and pretended to spank her.

That reminds me of when my dad spanked me a few times. I was not always the best-behaved boy in the world. I usually did little things wrong. My mother insisted only a few times that my dad spank me. He would put me over his lap, this was when I was little, and gently jar me with his huge hand. He would tell me to pretend to cry for my mother. I think we quit that charade when I was about six years old. I remember my mother smiling. She knew what was going on.

You both were so easy to rear. I'm not sure if I even gave either one of you a serious disciplinary talk, and you never really changed. You have always done few things wrong, nothing bad at all. The only time I had to correct you with a talk might have been about cheating at games or too vigorously arguing a point of view. I, however, will have to admit that little lies crept into your way of life at an early age. You started exaggerating things a little bit also. I think you started blurring the line between truth and lies maybe without knowing it. It didn't seem a big thing at first, but later I began thinking it might be a problem. I truly believe that you are a very well behaved person. You are a special wonderful person, exceptional indeed. If that changes, it will not be your entire fault. I will blame it on your upbringing experiences. I wish I could have had a better chance to help raise you. I wished for more time in the past and now more time with you in the future. I hope it isn't too late for me to have more quality time with you.

Sincerely,

Dad

Knife Penetration

I spent too
much time
trying to win
your heart
it seems, for in
my seemingly
wasted effort,
misconception was
born.
Out of darkness
came untruths that
I could not battle.

Where in grace can
I find tomorrow?
Will I have to
let tomorrow
find me in grace?

What else can
I do to
defend myself
except to offer
my back again.
Might I have to
accept knife
penetration again if
disorder seeks chaos?
I pray that not be
your decision or
my destiny.

Dear Angela – *Time Well Spent*

I don't regret not letting other things in my life distract from time with you and Kaitlyn. There was always the fear that someone was going to steal one or both of you. That idea helped spur me to spend as much time with you as possible. The resulting years proved that I was correct in my time preservation. I could have done other work and gotten more money for us, but I refused. I could have coached again, but that would have taken time away. I could have participated in hobbies or other time consuming activities, but I chose to spend time with you girls.

When remembering back, I regret not one moment spent with you girls. I have learned that time is the most precious thing we deal with every day. Time is all we finally have or do not have. I thank God for every moment that I had with you and Kaitlyn. Thank you for your time given. I hope we can have much more time for yet a long time. Please allow me into your life.

I wish I had spent more time with my other two children. When a person is young and poor, they have different priorities than when older. I taught school, coached and worked during the summer time when younger. I wish I had been a better father to Brook and Kristen. They, however, think I was and am still a good father. They were and are yet great people. I wish you knew them better.

I well remember our walks in all seasons on the "Spring Falls" property and Jenny's "Rock River Farm" property. Did you know the name of our place was Spring Falls, named after the creek that flowed in a horseshoe shape on and off our property? Remember when we would go down to the so-called beach. We played in the water and sand. That was a cool place.

Do you remember how the creek would rise and roar when a big rain occurred? We could hear it from the house that was quite a distance away. It would sometimes rise to the bottom of the bridge. It, however, didn't take long to get shallow again.

That creek flows into Sugar Creek, which flows into the Wabash River. Our cabin, as you know, is on the Wabash River. Theoretically, we could canoe from that spot to the cabin.

We could, if having a mind to, also take our flat bottom river boat all the way to New Orleans and the Gulf of Mexico by going down the Wabash to the Mississippi and then to the Gulf. I might put that trip on my *bucket list*. You do see the word "might."

We used to throw rocks into Spring Falls Creek when I lived at Jenny's house and make a wish for each rock thrown. I always wished for the same thing, and that was that you would come live with me. We threw many rocks in that creek and made many wishes. I wonder how many of your wishes came true. Of course, my habitual wish didn't have much chance of coming true.

Do you remember that year when Earl Luzader told us about the baby vultures in the hollow tree trunk? We followed the path and found the tree on Jenny's property. We gazed inside that big tree hole and scared the momma vulture. We had no idea that she was in her nest. She was huge and came out in a hurry, scaring the peewadden out of us. She scared us more than we scared her.

We ran away startled for a few feet and then went back to see the two young vultures. The mamma vulture watched and stared at us from a high tree branch. We were afraid she would fly down and scratch our eyes out, but she didn't. She only gave us that scary menacing stare. We went back to the nest many times that summer. The baby vultures got bigger quickly. One of them hissed at us and pretended to be aggressive, but the other one stayed quietly in a fearful bundle of immature feathers.

Spring Falls was a better place to live for me than Jenny's Rock River Farm. It was nice to stay at Jenny's after the divorce, but I preferred staying with you. It was convenient at Jenny's because we could walk across the road to visit.

I remember raking leaves and playing in them during fall. I remember making snowmen in winter. I remember collecting black walnuts, picking flowers and planting garden seeds and plants.

The seasons came and went. Flowers bloomed and snow fell. Walnuts fell and squirrels gathered them. Little black walnut trees sprouted from the earth from squirrel planted walnuts every year. God gives and takes away inflexibly according to His will. That is a tough thing to remember and accept with blind faith.

Only God knows His plan. I learned that a person can't ever get angry with God. In fact, it's downright stupid to get angry with God.

Sincerely,

Dad

Deciding Worth

A triangular glass piece,
half buried in black soil,
green glitters in sun,
draws attention today.
An old coke bottle part,
separated years ago,
waiting discovery.
Once a part of something
whole and useful,
it now seems to
serve no purpose.
It is treasure to someone,
trash to another.
It is gently pulled from earth,
washed clean,
ground and polished as
if a diamond.
It becomes a jewel as
corners are rounded and
edges are smoothed.
It is mounted in a
silver wire cradle,
placed on a delicate
beaded string and
hung around a
beautiful neck.
An old worthless
coke bottle piece
becomes an appreciated
loved jewel and
glitters in someone's eyes as
never thought possible.

How many broken glass pieces
lie waiting to be found,
polished and transformed
into a cherished jewel?
How many willing artists can
smooth and bring glitter to
someone's eyes?
There is an artist bit in
all who can humbly search
earth's gritty soil and
find treasures hiding
beneath surface black.

Dear Angela – *Paths*

Do you remember those paths that I cut through the woods? I originally followed deer paths when clearing them. It was a lot of work cutting out trees and cleaning up fallen brush. There were also bushes, weeds and vines to clear. I finally cleared several paths and each had a special stopping place to meditate. I named each deliberating place. I can't remember but two of them now. I remember "the valley," where we could sit on a log and look down into a deep ravine. Another place, "the church," where a big tree had fallen onto a smaller tree and bent it down while it further grew. It remained bowed downward like a cathedral arch after I removed the big tree. We later put a cross there and pretended it was a church. Do you remember going there and praying?

I remember one time when I was at the church place, thinking and meditating. I looked a few feet from where sitting and saw a huge morel mushroom. It was about eight inches tall. I was amazed. I then looked about five feet farther and saw another giant mushroom. I took them as a sign that things were going to be all right. I had found very few mushrooms that spring, and had found nothing like those two big beauties.

One other time I found a lone small purple flower that looked like miniature grapes at the church place. I hadn't seen anything like it before and have not since. It was growing an inch or so from the cross. I picked it, dried it and took it to school. My science teacher friend could not identify it. I placed it on Kaitlyn's ash box. It is there with our mementoes yet today. I took the wild flower also as a sign. I was beginning to see, but not understand signs. I yet look for signs. Do you think I'm crazy?

I remember one time we were back in the woods and heard a loud noise coming from a distant path. Buddy, who I also called Big Brown Dog, used to chase deer, but this time a deer was chasing him. I think the deer was protecting her fawn and, as you know, deer are very protective of their young. Well, Big Brown Dog was running as fast as he could down the path. His tucked rear end was down between his back legs. He was running close to the ground with the deer behind him, heading straight towards us. She broke-off the chase when seeing us standing on the trail. I was beginning to wonder what to do if they continued running towards us. I certainly considered grabbing you and running to get out of the way. Fortunately, the deer was more afraid of us than Big Brown Dog. I thought it amusing later, but at the time of the chase, it was scary. Big Brown Dog, however, didn't learn his lesson. He was back chasing deer the next day.

Sincerely,

Dad

Consoling Bells

Gone are standard bells
forged in primal sleep,
arranged in cosmic dust,
gathered a billion years ago.

Modern weavers created a
blanket on which I fly,
avoiding sleep all together.
Unlike an old worn bell
that has lost its ring,
I cherish time and
remember own tone.

Where are white winged
angels who lived quality
time in glorious towers?
I cannot feel them.
I fear they have gone to
someone else's frequently
unsettled mind.

I am tolling a message as
I fly my blanket over a
bewildered world.
Can you hear my voice in
valleys folding or in
mountains staging?

Some say time is short, but
I think it is long, and
humanity must endure for a
long restraining time.

Get your own flying blanket,
fly to where it is safe.
Ride magnetic waves and
crystal vibrations.
Be your own
consoled warning bell.

Dear Angela – *Good Times*

I remember Freckles getting caught in an abandoned barbed wire fencerow in the woods. I think her name was Mollie, our other dog, that came to the house and then led us to Freckles. I followed Mollie back into the woods not knowing what she wanted.

Freckles was quietly lying, waiting for us to rescue her. I carefully untangled her from the barbed wire. She patiently waited, trusting me, knowing I was rescuing her. She seemed totally exhausted. I guessed that she had spent much time trying to free herself. I carried her all the way back to the house. It's funny, that once I got her back to the house and laid her on the grass, she got up and took off running. I think she was milking the situation and my attention. I was glad to have helped her and knew she appreciated it, but I think she took advantage of me. She was a smart dog.

Sometimes I forget how good life was during that time. The good thing is that I was aware of that wonderful time passing. There have been times when life was and wasn't what I wanted. However, I was usually happy and aware of time. I am yet that way, happy and aware of passing time. I am blessed. I never forget that.

Sincerely,

Dad

Unimportant

Some unimportant
things become
part of something
important.
Some important
things
are unique and
obscure, but
functional.
A bolt
by itself is
only a bolt, but
with a nut it
becomes a fastener.
A tree
among many
becomes a forest.
One of a hundred
fallen walnuts will
someday become a tree.

Tree legacy
lives for tomorrow, each
leaf, each nut is
part of a whole, and thus
part of an evolutionary forest.
How then can one
human being be different?

How then can one
visit beyond heaven
be unimportant?

A spiritual visit to
earth from heaven is a
part of many visits.
It is part of
something bigger and
more important.
It becomes a
spiritual legacy of God.
Each visit is part of a
total spiritual experience
making up a complete
spiritual fastening whole, and
like trees and nuts,
it is complicated made
simple through unimportance.

A human being is
seemingly unimportant to a
collective whole and
important to a
unique individual, yet a
reverse principle is at work;
spirits are part of a whole,
on earth as in heaven, thus are
fasteners of God,
securing human existence.
A spirit by itself has
little function and
can do little good, but
with other spirits,
it can accomplish
great mankind feats.
Humanity is important.

*One spiritual piece of
God is an ultimate
important piece of a
whole evolving universe.
A forest without trees is
no forest.
A machine without
bolts cannot
be assembled.
Importance without
unimportance
has no spiritual legacy,
no future,
no purpose.*

CHAPTER IV

Life
Understanding

Dear Angela – *September 21*

It was the night of September 21 when I heard you and Kaitlyn talking after going to bed. I lay awake listening, but couldn't hear any particular words, only a soft seemingly private conversation. I went to sleep after about a half hour while you girls kept talking. I found it unusual, but not disturbing. Little did I know that Kaitlyn was preparing you for the future. She was communicating how your lives were about to change. In retrospect, I know this. Also in retrospect, I should have taken the conversation as a sign, but my ignorance of the spiritual world kept me unaware. It yet hammers away at my earthly stupidity and I still remain ignorant concerning the spiritual world.

You told me later that Kaitlyn said she was leaving and that you would be staying behind. I guess she even explained how she would pass. You gave me few details. I always wondered why you never told us, never warned us, but then you probably thought it was perfectly natural. You never said why you didn't tell us. You only said that Kaitlyn told you what was going to happen, but you could not tell us. Only after the fact did you tell us anything. I guess we would have tried to stop it if we had known. We were not supposed to know. Oh, I don't understand yet. All I can do is continue to have faith that everything was the will of God.

I understand so little about the spiritual world, but I do believe that Kaitlyn was educated very much in the subject and that she shared much of her wisdom with you. I think you have forgotten most of what she said or what you experienced. I am trying to review what I remember with you now.

I think you were allowed to know some spiritual knowledge and were told what you needed to know to endure what was about to happen. I think you have probably forgotten what you experienced; however, I think there are remnants within that guide you even today. You have spiritual understanding that is beyond most of us. I will never forget that night when you spoke quietly in that nearly dark room with only a dim nightlight glowing, where spiritual and earthly worlds met to reveal the future. My heart yet aches as I picture you girls lying on your backs next to each other discussing cosmic order.

My head hurts thinking about it now. I feel so helpless even now. I yet reach out for Kaitlyn. I now reach out to you.

I am here to share what little I know and remember. I truly believe that you received knowledge to help you cope with life and death, and that you understand it more than you know or wish to share.

Sincerely,

Dad

Control

Lily petals
fall silently
on rushing water,
like small boats
freely floating
downstream.

  Like trivial transports
  we are,
  carried carelessly, but
  constantly
  down life's
  precarious stream.

    From passively
    swimming
    mother's womb;
    we cry,
    scream and
    swim into our world.

      We take
      uncertain strokes
      toward destiny,
      accepting an
      insecure
      continuing journey.

        Like retreating petals
        falling, drifting and
        meandering,
        we perilously,
        spiritually float
        towards eternity.

Dear Angela – *September 27*

It was the evening of September 27 and Kaitlyn had a high temperature. It was three days after you and Kaitlyn started preschool. I believe a particular boy that she befriended at preschool exposed her to harmful bacteria. It is only a theory and I'm not blaming anyone for her getting sick. I do have information that leads me to this conclusion. I can't talk about it. I don't want to blame anyone because I believe it was her destiny to leave Earth when she did. There are many circumstances, or maybe we might call them forces, that led to her death.

Kaitlyn didn't get better after a few hours. The fever continued, so we called the doctor who was on call that night. Bill Leech was his name. He said to give her aspirin and see if that took the temperature down. It seemed to work some, but after an hour or so, her temperature rose again. Her temperature then climbed to around 102 degrees and remained at that number. We called Dr. Leech again and he said to watch her and see if the temperature got any higher. We did and the temperature remained at about 102 degrees.

We took Kaitlyn to bed with us. She lay next to me all night. She didn't sleep well. I didn't sleep at all. She lay restlessly next to me, half asleep I thought at the time. Her hot little sweaty body pressed against me all night. She was restless and anxious, which was not her natural temperament. Her tiny little heart pounded very fast and her breathing was fast, causing me to fear that she was very sick. I tried to comfort her all night, but with little success.

We called the doctor again about 3:00 am. He said she would be all right if her temperature stayed at or under 102 degrees, and keep giving her aspirin. We trusted him, but should not have. I will not go into why we should have mistrusted him at this point. Let me just say that he had other things on his mind other than a small child and desperate parents. I think he was too busy for us at one and three o-clock in the morning. I think he had jaded judgment. I think he later proved that he didn't have good judgment about many things. I'm not blaming him for Kaitlyn's death, but I think he didn't give us the best advice. I believe that he is probably a poor doctor. The only time we went back to his medical group was to seek out another doctor for you because your blood work numbers were not good.

We later found Dr. Scott Douglas, who I'm sure you remember, and he turned out to be God sent. He is smart, hardworking and highly patient concerned. He is yet my doctor. He stood in line once for several hours just to sign you up for a new vaccination. He used to sterilize a patient room for you before visiting his office. He also did studies on seasonal bacteria in his medical office to see when it was best for you to come for an appointment. He certainly went out of his way to accommodate us. I have high respect for him. You should always remember him with high esteem.

We kept giving Kaitlyn aspirin, but her temperature never came down until early morning. She seemed to have passed through the crisis because her temperature had seemingly peaked. She and I got up and ate breakfast together.

Angela, you slept the whole night and never questioned us about Kaitlyn being sick. You and Kaitlyn always slept together, always, yet you remained in a separate bed all night. You slept as if nothing was wrong. Kaitlyn and I finished our breakfast about the time Phil Cummins, our plumber, came to put in a new well pump and tank. He and I had worked on the new pump for a couple of hours before your mother came outside to talk. She said that Kaitlyn was sick again like the night before, except now she was lethargic. Your mother's parents were up from Florida. Forest said he would take your mother and Kaitlyn to the doctor. I stayed behind to help with the pump. I kissed Kaitlyn good-by, but hurriedly. I now wish I had taken longer, or even better, had taken her to the doctor myself.

About an hour later, your mother called and told me that the doctor said to take Kaitlyn to the hospital. He said there was nothing he could do for her in the office. About an hour later, your mother called again saying that I needed to come to the hospital.

I think I will quit now for a little while. I don't want to go on just now. I don't know why I can write about this now anyway. I've tried before with no real success. It has been over fourteen years, but most of what I'm writing about seems like yesterday. Apparently, some part of my psyche accepts many years of thinking, reasoning and healing. The mind is a wonderful thing, but the spirit is a magnificent extension of God. I could not have worked my way through life, especially this part of my life, without the Holy Spirit's help.

He even helps me now to write this book, that's for sure. Maybe I'm able to write about Kaitlyn now because our relationship has changed. The fear of losing you figures into my courage concerning being able to write our story about and with Kaitlyn. I don't mean I fear your death. I fear losing you on earth, not in heaven. I fear I'll not see you for a long time. I yet love you so much.

Sincerely,

Dad

Inside Outward

My hands are
rough and
worn as is
soul and
rendered letters.
My face is
wrinkled and a
bit leathery as is
battered soul.
My hair is
gray and a
bit thin as is
weathered mind, and
sculpted philosophy.

I run not so
fast or think so
quickly and yet
I don't care much
in these later years
about such things.
I'm not running
towards, but
away from
challenge and
ego mounting.

Beneath my
rough exterior a
smooth soul
resides and a
known spirit that
follows a new path
each day.

Maps and charts
I shuffled with
worn hands,
waning mind and
dimming eyes.

It is strange how
I see and
feel much better
now, as if from
inside outward,
rather than
outside inward.

My world is
now smaller,
dreams more real,
life shorter.
I remember
many things as if
yesterday occurred.
All I can do now is
recall and explain,
share and teach,
live and die.

One Man's Test

I seek no other way than
basking in early sunlight.
Leafy spring trees dance outside
my morning window,
casting shadows, decorating walls
before my fascinated eyes.
I am morning driven like a
flower reaching, tree needing,
like nature teaching,
teaching, teaching.
There is no better nourishment
than silent morning time.
My sun decorated walls are like
Rorschach ink images.
My positive opinions are
like those trees micro growing,
growing, growing,
then like death decaying,
decaying, decaying.
I shall be a tree,
growing inside outward,
casting wall shadows to
be studied by another
needing awareness.
If it be so, then
my purpose is
like shadow casting,
revealing and accepting,
accepting, accepting.

Dear Angela – *September 28*

I went directly to the hospital emergency waiting room and someone directed me to a special room where your mother was waiting.

She grabbed me when I entered the room and said, "She's gone, she's gone."

I didn't understand at first. I couldn't imagine what she was saying. She held onto me while crying, and repeated the words, "She's gone."

It then soaked in that Kaitlyn was dead.

"No, no," was all I could say. I pretended to hear incorrectly. "No, no, that can't be."

I finally accepted the words, but not the reality. I could not stand. Your mother and I hung to each other, bracing each other. I could not speak, but I mumbled, "No, no." I could not understand, could not even try. Everything became a blur. Your mother went into detail about how Kaitlyn got worse and how they did everything possible to save her in the emergency room. She told me how Kaitlyn sat up and said that she loved your mother. She then lay back down and never said another word. She said that Kaitlyn went very fast. She said more things in detail, but right then nothing mattered except Kaitlyn was gone. I heard few of her words.

We went to the emergency room where Kaitlyn still laid on the emergency room bed. She was white, lifeless. All that colorful beauty was gone and only precious white remained. Her face was, as I now reflect, that same white color as the Riley Hospital clown's face that I saw in the photo many months ago.

I saw nothing else but Kaitlyn and couldn't think of anything else but Kaitlyn at the time. I touched her stillness. I gazed at her whiteness and studied her black, completely dilated eyes that were yet open. I couldn't accept her passing. I couldn't accept reality. I never felt such mental or physical pain before or after those few minutes of agony that seemed like hours. I had knife pain in my chest. I was sick at my stomach. My head was about to explode.

I can't explain the worst thing that ever happened to me in my life. I can't explain to you or anyone. Only those who have gone through it can understand. I wish I knew if you understand what I'm writing. I wish you could explain how you felt then and feel now.

There will never be another experience as painful as Kaitlyn's death, and that includes my own death. I shall not try to explain to you my limitations. I think you understand more about what happened to Kaitlyn than I do. I think you have forgotten much of what you went through, what you experienced and how you reacted to her death. I think God blessed and taught you through Jesus about Kaitlyn's passing.

I believe Kaitlyn prepared you that night in bed a week before her passing. I think she explained what was going to happen and why. I think you both understood what it meant to pass from earthly presence to heavenly presence. I wish you could teach me.

I believe even though you have forgotten much, there are shared knowledge remnants that allow you to understand her passing. We have talked about it some, but that was a long time ago. We have not shared our feelings. I wonder if you have talked to your mother or to one of your friends about your feelings. I fear I have been a poor dad and friend. I want to do better. I hope it is not too late.

Sincerely,

Dad

Ash and Stone

I silently sit in a
melancholy place,
recalling flowers and
how they transform into
ash and stone.

I wish to better caress
in forgiving ways,
practice God's instructions,
give love and planting
spiritual awareness.

I wish to pray ahead
in morning light and
speak "I love you"
in night's darkness for
I have fallen short.

I wish to portend
details while cultivating
family grain and allow
golden soulful wheat to
wave well until harvest.

Flowers on a casket lay,
September 28, 1996 while
sleeping wheat waits, and
I tearfully, ruefully
ash and stone transplant.

Dear Angela – *Euphoria*

You slept until wakened about nine o-clock the morning Kaitlyn passed. You slept through the whole ordeal. You slept while Kaitlyn got worse during the night and while being taken to the hospital where she died. You slept through her passing.

You seemed to be all right with everything. You danced and sang when they brought you to the hospital. I have never seen you happier, before or after her passing. I can't help but think you knew exactly what was happening. I can't help but think you knew she was in heaven, a place of pure love and joy. I think you knew she wouldn't have to suffer that which was in her future. I pray you will not have to endure more than is fair.

I believe that Kaitlyn told you what was in her future. I think you either slept through what happened to her or experienced it with her while sleeping. Either way, you danced and sang at the hospital, which you rarely did, as if taking on some of Kaitlyn's personality traits. She liked to sing and dance and now you were doing the same.

You seemed to be in a euphoric state of mind for several hours until adults showed you how to "supposedly" feel and act. I think it was a wonderful event for you and a horrible passing for us. I think you soon realized what was earthly happening. I don't know which realization is better at a funeral, heavenly knowledge or earthly reality, but I do know which one was better for you at the time. Maybe it's all a matter of circumstance. Maybe it's all a matter of understanding. I believe that you received enough wisdom to get you through the ordeal and most of it was temporary. Only you can tell me differently.

I think you probably remember little about Kaitlyn's passing. You probably remember little of the given knowledge. I wish to talk to you about it someday, but I'm not sure it would be in your best interest. I believe that it is private knowledge for you and none of my business. If I had a need to know, I would have received more knowledge.

I was given some wisdom, but of course not enough for my satisfaction. I'll write about a conversation we had concerning your given wisdom later.

Sincerely,

Dad

Last Candle

She burned
last candle,
used last match,
slept beside sister
one last time
while night
prevailed, while
wafting ceiling fan
rushed air over
innocent bodies
near last time.

She morning laid
like a silent
Easter Island statue,
half buried in sand,
waiting for
someone to take
her home.

o

I felt
spiritual beings
gather my arms and
pull me
upward as if
I also was in heavy sand.

I gained legs
to walk,
to run,
to explore
her island with
zeal.

I groped in
darkness for days.
It was strange
how a moon-less night
sought no wisdom and a
mind-less world
desired no relief.

o

She fumbled in
darkness and
found a candle,
then a match.
Her dark world
became lighted
again with
instant flash of
holiness.

She stood with
outstretched arms,
gave a knock at
heaven's door and
stood with
outstretched arms.

She saw
guiding Easter Island
counterpart,
holding an ancient
glowing tablet and
he took hand,
kissed cheek and
held her for a
long time.

o

I also groped
no longer for
match or
candle, and
in my soul
rose a light and a
love that would
last forever.

Somehow
wisdom eroded
me free and
washed sand from
my essence.
I ran towards
truth and
it consoled.

Dear Angela – *Prayers*

Do you know how we got started attending Christ Lutheran Church? Well, we would drive by the church while turning onto highway 32 going towards home. Kaitlyn mentioned very often that she wanted to go inside that church.

She later said, "I want to go to that church."

We finally attended the church and then went back repeatedly. We became regulars and your mother was involved with VBS. You and Kaitlyn liked VBS very much. I helped with it one year. We always said that Kaitlyn got us involved with religion and Christ Lutheran Church.

I grew up infrequently attending a Baptist church. I later went to First Baptist Church in Crawfordsville. I was baptized there with full immersion. Baptizing wasn't the emotional or spiritual experience I thought it would be. I was spiritually unaffected. I later found myself more moved by God after I got a divorce from Kristen's and Brook's mother.

That was a time when I greatly needed God. I think He spoke to me and showed me how to mend myself. He then partially taught me how to be patient. My spirituality has been growing ever since that time. It accelerated when Kaitlyn passed. I yet am growing spiritually. I am yet learning about God through the Holy Spirit who is my friend, adviser and counselor.

I had a conversation with Pastor Stacy about a week before Kaitlyn passed.

I said, "I don't know what to pray for because my life is nearly perfect. I have my family, job and house. My wife has her stables and horses. My girls have a wonderful place in which to grow. I even have my car, truck and mini farm paid for."

He answered, "Then pray for those who don't have much."

Therefore, I did for about a week until the playing field leveled. Everything positive seemed to be equalized with one gigantic negative event. The world would never be the same for me. I had to learn to pray a different way and for different things.

I had to pray for help and understanding. I had to pray for my family and for you, Angela. I prayed that I would somehow see Kaitlyn again, even though, I knew it wouldn't happen.

However, "knowing," what is that really? Lack of faith was what it was then, lack of faith. There are no "no possibilities" when one has faith.

I believe that God told me to keep my heart and mind open. I remember when I found out that you also didn't have a spleen, I prayed for two years that Jesus would give you my spleen or the remnant you had would grow into a complete spleen. That never happened. It would have been a miracle for us, but only a small thing for Jesus. Anyway, I had to learn to pray all over again. I had to pray for different things.

When I finally realized what kind of prayers to present and let the Holy Spirit translate to God, they came down to "thank you prayers," not "asking" prayers. I learned to thank God for my blessings and to protect those I loved. It's strange how tragedy opens one's mind.

I yet pray asking prayers, but ask for different things. I pray *The Mantra of Jabez*. There is a book by Bruce Wilkinson that explains it. I pray it every day when I finish my swimming. I ask at the same time for the Lord to watch over all of us, especially my children and grandchildren, and especially, especially you, Angela. I pray a thank-you prayer nearly every night before I fall asleep for all that I am thankful and all He has given me. I pray when I look at the picture of you and Kaitlyn that sits on her oak ash remains box. I am looking at it now. It is a picture when you were about three years old. I also now frequently give a thank you prayer in the morning when I wake up for being here another day.

Sincerely,

Dad

Dear Angela – *Advice*

I did keep my heart and mind open. I did get help and advice from a higher power. I believe He spoke to me. I think it was the second time that God spoke to me.

The other time was when I was much younger and ignorantly in a deep black hopeless pit.

He told me, "Look up, see that pinpoint of light. That is the way out of the pit." He also said, "Start climbing. I am with you."

The second time He spoke to me was when I needed it most.

He said, "You were blessed with Kaitlyn and Angela. Kaitlyn was a blessing for three and half years. Spend as much time with Angela as you can."

He gave me this advice when alone in the woods. I could go to that very spot right now. Sorrow and pain permeated my body and mind. I had this horrible pain in my chest. I could only look downward. It was difficult to look anyone in the eye.

God also said, "Three and a half years is long enough to live a perfect life."

I then went on to reason for myself that length of life does not matter so much. Would I want a perfect short life or a long unsatisfactory life? Earth life length, whether conceived long or short, matters not when measuring success. I believe that Kaitlyn had a very influential successful perfect life.

She made an impact on the world. I hope that I further her impact by writing this book. You can further affect her world, Angela, with your success. I believe Kaitlyn helped you enter the world and continues to watch over you. She is your guardian angel. She is yet with both of us.

I believe that she watched over Brook immediately after she died. Brook was in too big of a hurry to get to Crawfordsville when Kaitlyn died. He was driving his truck on Interstate 75 in the rain when a van pulled over in front of him. He swerved and lost control of his truck. He totaled his truck. They treated him for minor cuts and scrapes at the hospital. He said he was lucky to be alive. I guess God figured that it would be just too much for me to lose two children within the same week, or to lose two children at all. Brook was without a vehicle and didn't make it to the funeral. He kept apologizing for not attending the funeral. I told him don't worry about it. I suspect he yet remembers not making it to the funeral.

I said, "You were probably Kaitlyn's first assignment as a guardian angel. She was looking out for you."

He agreed by saying, "Someone for sure was looking out for me."

I think most ministers say that we earthly mortals don't turn into angels, but I'm not so sure. I think there are angels and spirits everywhere. I believe that the spiritual world is all around us. Earth probably gets a little crowded with all the angels moving around protecting us. I surely hope so. I would rather give the spiritual world and the Holy Spirit too much credit than not enough.

Sometimes I wish to pass into the spiritual world without dying to experience its awesome dimensions. I have felt this way for a long time. I especially have felt this way since Kaitlyn passed. I have also thought, however, that it surely is a place of good and evil, good and bad spirits, and angels and demons. I ask myself whether I truly want to experience the dark side of the spiritual world. Do I have the courage to know and fight the dark side? Maybe in my own quiet way, I already fight evil. Maybe we all encounter it, resist it and fight it. Some give in to the dark side. Some people sell their souls to the devil. Who knows from where evil comes. Of course, the religious belief is that the devil is a fallen angel. I believe that the devil exists, that evil exists and I am susceptible to it every day.

We must, you must look out for those who will lead you astray. There are humans who work for the devil and might well be possessed by the devil rather than indwelled by the Holy Spirit. "Be aware of a wolf in sheep's clothing," so it is said.

Sincerely,

Dad

Pretending

Life's secret is pretending to
be something not.
No one is something without
desire, confidence and effort.
One must first pretend to be
something, then and only then,
does one chance to be something.
Few truly become something special.
Most strive to become whether
teacher, preacher or musician.
No one was born something except
ignorant, inept or enslaved.
One has to pretend, for in this
pretentiousness comes a true
believer, deceiver or captain.
Ultimate pretentiousness is
being Christ, for one can never
be Christ, only a little Christ-like.
One must pretend to watch,
coach or play ball.
There's no chance to become
without confidence to become.
Never let anyone know
pretending is happening or
know accomplishment is incomplete.
One must pretend in order to
become, pretend in order to be.

Dear Angela – *Holy Spirit*

I pretended to be ok and went back to school one week after Kaitlyn died, but I went through hell and heaven during that week. I experienced earthly pain and heavenly pleasure. I was slowly mending after the first acceptance moment of her passing. God spoke to me through the Holy Spirit. I've come to love and rely on Him for advice, guidance and knowledge. I read the book, *The Promise* by Tony Evans about a year after Kaitlyn died. It changed me and gave new spiritual perspective to my life. Mr. Evans taught me about the Holy Spirit and showed me how He is involved in my life every day, all day.

Anyway, back to returning to work. I think it helped me get through the ordeal, even though, it was very difficult. It was tough being around your mother. She was on the telephone eight hours a day, telling her story. I guess we all have our ways of dealing with tragedy. I withdrew within myself as she escaped outward. I'm more of an introvert and she, an extrovert. I talked to other people, but they couldn't help. Pastor Stacy had no real answers. My religious friend, Ramon Garrett, didn't have answers. No one could tell me why she had to leave this earth so soon.

Only the Holy Spirit counseled me. He became my best friend, and remains my best friend and spiritual adviser. Debi is my best friend concerning earthly relationships. I reached out to you, but I think you had your own counsel. I think you had Jesus and Kaitlyn to help you through the ordeal. I think Kaitlyn, as her true spiritual self, remained here on earth for a while, helping us all, but you specially.

Sincerely,

Dad

Flowers than Weeds

I placed
here and there
those things that
made me cry,
planted them
widely without
thought as if in a
garden so large
I could not
see other side.
And now as
I stroll that garden,
seldom seeing
anything
sorrow growing.
Only flora
mutations do
I see that
appear more
like
flowers than
weeds.

Dear Angela – *Blurry Mind*

We had the funeral a few days after September 28. I'm not sure what day it was because everything was hazy and my mind didn't work so well. Even now, it's all quite blurry. I spent time with you, family and friends, but was separated by my grief. We were together, but separate in time and space, here and there and at different emotional levels. Sometimes I wish I could do it over and get it right the next time, but I couldn't stand the pain again, and besides, there is no real way of doing it right.

All people can do is follow their instincts and hopefully receive guidance from others who have suffered a similar ordeal. I met a few people who had lost a child or grandchild at a very early age. I taught school with Larry Pile who lost his son at around age 18. Dick and Elaine Trout lost a grandchild very early in life. Helen Hudson, who I also taught with, lost her son at 18. I could mention more, but it's not necessary for you also know people who have lost a child. Many of those people also had children who know the loss of a sibling. I can only imagine your pain, losing a sister, a twin sister. I wish we could talk about it. There are many more people who have lost children than I realized. I was certainly not alone. I didn't need to watch TV to know it happens every day.

That, however, does not lessen the pain. It just gives a better understanding of life and death. Others who had lost a child at an early age couldn't convey their thoughts and emotions to me with words, but one long look into their eyes and the expression on their face was all I needed for understanding. I couldn't convey my thoughts and feelings to you then, Angela. You were so young. I think I could now since you are nearly grown up and I have found time and distance from that rueful day. I have found solace in my heart, mind and soul.

I remember much of the funeral through a warm and blurry mind. Kaitlyn lay in a small cremating casket. It was open and I could see her beautiful white face and could almost believe that she would sit up, and climb out of the box. That of course was impossible, but my mind wished it so and nearly believed it possible. You sat with us up front during the funeral. Three women from the church sang three songs from Vacation Bible School, which had taken place just a few weeks previously.

Someone sang *Amazing Grace*, which I had requested. That song yet stirs deep emotion to this day and makes my eyes water when played or sung. I remember the funeral and many details even if it was a dark day. Pastor Stacy tried to explain why and how her passing made sense and satisfy many other questions. Nothing made sense until God spoke to me out there in the woods a few days later.

He said those few words to me through the Holy Spirit. "She was a blessing. You had three and a half wonderful years with her."

I finally agreed, especially realizing how so many children are leaving this world by evil hands. Jesus took Kaitlyn. I can nearly see her walking hand in hand with Jesus in heaven.

I think she is with my mother and dad. She is with others who have passed before her. I believe she plays with Martha Bennett, Debi's sister, who drowned at age 18 months in their family farm pond. I think she has talked with Debi's mother, Betty, about Martha's passing. Betty just passed a couple months ago. I think she has met with my friend Steve Swick, the tough Viet Nam Army veteran and Green Beret soldier, who passed away at age 56. Oh, there is no end to those she has met in heaven. I think she is yet extroverted even in heaven.

What do you think? I believe there are many people waiting on me in heaven. I think it will be great when I get there, but I'm in no big hurry. I think I have much to do here before leaving.

Speaking of things to do, I have several books that are near finished and ready to publish. I figured the other day that I have at least 5,000 more days to live and every day has the potential for success. I plan to live to be 85. Don't you think that is reasonable?

I plan to publish several more books, travel and visit with family and friends. I have my bucket list. I cross off one item every once in a while and write in a new one. I guess I will never complete the bucket list. I think that's a good thing.

I once heard someone ask another, "What is the most exciting thing you ever did?"

The person answered, "I hope I haven't done it yet."

Now that is my kind of answer. That is my kind of attitude..

Sincerely,

Dad

Melancholy

Melancholy is
self-reflection.
Some weeping is
necessary.

True melancholy is
liberating.
Melancholy is
not depressing.

Its fuel for
soul.
Introspection causes
living history.

Wish to sing a
melancholy song.
Feel better from
sadness.

Crying is for a
reason.
Tears wash clean
own history.

That is why
they invented blues.
Everyone remembers
good and bad times..

Dear Angela – *Oak Box*

Kaitlyn's cremated ashes are in a small oak box, which I yet have at my house. We agreed to wait until you were older and then all of us could decide what to do with her ashes. I found out that there are not so many ashes in the box. Debi's mother had many ashes when cremated. Her box was quite heavy. I reasoned that Kaitlyn was so small that she had few ashes. I had not given that thought before. Kaitlyn even had several mementoes put into her casket. We put her American Girl doll in the casket. Do you still have your American Girl doll? I remembered the doll because Ava just got one. She showed it to me when I was visiting Kristen and her family in Denver just a couple weeks ago.

I go to that oak ash box often. It reminds me of much. I often wonder if you need a place for communion with Kaitlyn. You never showed an interest in the oak box when visiting. Why is that when it means so much to me? Maybe I'm just earthly stupid. Someday soon I think, we should decide what to do with her ashes. I think there should be a permanent place for them. What do you think?

Well, you are certainly older and we haven't decided. I don't mind keeping the ashes at all, but feel that I should share them. I think they need a final resting place so others can also reach out to Kaitlyn. I once thought you would want to lay at rest in the same place as Kaitlyn, but then I realized that you have a life of your own. I thought Crawfordsville would be the place for Kaitlyn's ashes because that was where she spent her whole life. Of course, you spent only about five years there. See, you already have a distinct life of your own.

You probably remember little about your days in Crawfordsville except when visiting me, not time living with Kaitlyn. Well, someday we will decide. Some day someone will have to decide about my ashes also. Wow, I have many people waiting for me up there. I don't think they will ask about my ashes.

Maybe I am gaining some wisdom about life and death after all. I want my body cremated, put in a nice oak box and buried in the cemetery at Farmersburg, Indiana with most of my family. There, now that's out of the way.

I, however, believe that Kaitlyn is not in that box, as I will not be in my oak box, but I do think such things might provoke our spiritual return. Sometimes I feel Kaitlyn is present when I rub and polish the box, speaking to her as if she were there. Maybe that is a little crazy, but then are not we all a little crazy?

I believe that we are spiritual beings and only occupy this earthly body for a short time. I also think Kaitlyn might help and watch over you occasionally. I think I mentioned that before. I know she did in some ways during the following months after she passed. I doubt that you remember her visits with you. I think she was with you several times after her passing. I will talk about that at another time.

Maybe sometime soon we can talk about where to put Kaitlyn's ashes. I think Crawfordsville would be the right place. There's a cemetery close to Christ Lutheran Church. I went to Christ Church a few times after you and your mother left town. I didn't want to go there for a couple of years. It just didn't feel right. Debi and I went there a few times before we moved to Lafayette. We both liked it there except for one particular person, whom I will not discuss.

We really liked Pastor Lowell Anderson, the interim pastor after Pastor Stacy retired. We liked his vision of a church. Of course, he wasn't there to change anything, just be a caretaker of the church.

He had experience, humility and spirituality. He gave much spiritual knowledge in bits and pieces. He got right to the point with few words. He caused me to think, meditate and learn. He led me to heavenly knowledge that I believe connects us all by and through the Holy Spirit. Does that make sense to you? I know we have differences about how God works.

Sincerely,

Dad

We Begin and End

We begin and end little,
destroying ourselves while
crying and dying,
naked and humble.

0

We end alone and
speechless while
beauty is gauged by
time, effort and result for
continued breathing only
brings life's joy.

Pursuing life's creation is
our purpose for in
our seed emerges a
spark hot enough to
ignite life's piled kindling
no matter stacked height.

0

So come and go with
grace and ease,
you'll never forget from where
you came and shall return.

Dear Angela – *Acceptance*

I doubt that you remember now because I spoke to you about this a couple of years after it happened and you didn't then remember. I will write about it for you.

It was about three weeks after Kaitlyn passed and we were walking in the woods behind the house. We were conversing about Kaitlyn's passing and about that night you two were talking in bed. It was about a week before the 28th or the day she passed. You told me that she talked about leaving, and that she was going to die and go to heaven. You didn't want to talk about it at that time and I didn't want to pry into your private knowledge. I felt as if you were not supposed to talk about it. I didn't press you about it, but encouraged you to talk. I had no idea what was going on in your mind. You did tell me that you went to heaven.

You said, "I saw Kaitlyn playing with other kids in heaven." You told me that you spoke with Jesus. I asked you what he said. You told me that He said, "I accept you."

I asked if you knew what that meant.

You told me, "He accepts me for what I am, but I will have to stay on earth for awhile."

I asked how long you were going to stay on earth, but you didn't have an answer. You then indicated that you didn't want to talk about it anymore. I respected your wishes. I have often thought about the words spoken to you by Jesus, "I accept you."

If I could hear just one word from Jesus, it would be "acceptance." I would need no other explanation concerning the hereafter. With you, I feel that I have an eyewitness to heaven's existence. I have no argument. I have no need for further proof. For sure, you were at the time a purely innocent being, free of corruption or false information and religious education. You were distinctly open for heavenly knowledge translation. I need little else to satisfy my faith. You gave me a wonderful gift. Thank you, Angela.

We didn't talk about it again until about two years later and at that time you couldn't remember what we talked about previously, and couldn't give me a definition of the word "accepts." I think God gave you some temporary information to get you through the ordeal of losing Kaitlyn. Then again, maybe you just didn't want to talk about it and that was your way of blowing me off. I yet believe that Jesus did speak with you. I believe in the hereafter more because I believe you were an eyewitness to heaven. I think you did go to heaven during that time when sleeping, while Kaitlyn was dying. I believe that you knew how wonderful heaven was, and that was why you were happy for several hours at and after the hospital.

I think you were an eyewitness to her passing and were in on the whole thing. I just wish you could remember more now. Even if you remember little, I think the Holy Spirit touched you. I think you are holy and have an old soul that knows more than most. I also believe that because you are good and spiritual, that the devil is at work in your life. He hates good and wants to conquer those who are good. Please be careful concerning those about you. Be smart, vigilant and unafraid.

You're susceptible to Satan and he would like nothing better than to make trouble for you. I think your mother and Terry are also vulnerable. I wish I could help you more.

Sincerely,

Dad

Speechless

Did you speak my name,
sitting quietly nearby or did
I imagine your voice
through thick silence and
unfiltered night light?

Did you think loudly,
making my mind vibrate or did
I only feel my own lazy blood
traveling neck artery
towards ignorant brain?

Did your hand extend,
making a lonesome gesture or did
I assume your sweet touch and
assurance that you were well and
would live forever that night?

Did you say good-night too soon,
extinguishing light or did
you never reach, never touch,
never turn that light on in
my heart, mind and soul?

Did you die wordlessly yesterday,
making a dark home place or did
you leave too soon while
awakening my God piece with
your silent disappearing beauty?

Angels Weep

Angels seldom
weep for
they know
what is and
how life
goes on.
But sometimes
even angels
have broken
hearts.
A spilled cup
cannot again
fill itself.
Even desperate
ghosts have
rights.
Someone must
accept an
apology for
fear haunts and
silence threatens.

Dear Angela – *Speaking of Mice*

I just got back from visiting Kristen's in Colorado and that reminded me of the mouse problem I had when first living at Jenny's farmhouse. I tried traps, but the place remained infested. There were just too many of them and they were reproducing like crazy. I resorted to poison and that finally did the job.

Well, Kristen had the same problem. She was catching mice and cleaning up mouse poop constantly. It was a health hazard. They live right on that greenway you know, so the mice are close and looking for a warm place to live in the fall. They chose houses along the greenway. I told her the only way to stop the problem, because she was infested, was to put out poison. Well, we did and it took care of the problem.

She put out poison again this year once Ethan said he heard a mouse. It is working again. She thanked me repeatedly. Of course, we put the poison where Bode, their dog, couldn't get to it and eat it. She said, "thank you" many times last year and again this year. I certainly remember that dirty mouse problem at Jenny's, but that was about the only drawback there at that beautiful place.

When Deb Cedars' American Red Ball moving men helped us move, one of them commented, "It would take a crowbar to pry me away from this place."

He was certainly thinking it a beautiful place to live.

I pointed at Debi and said, "Well, there is the little crowbar standing over there."

I was certainly glad we got help moving to Lafayette. Deb Cedars told me to keep the drawers loaded with clothing and his men would just move the furniture, drawers and all. Well, I left them full. The only thing is that the oak bedroom furniture that I designed and constructed myself was very heavy. I used to take out the drawers when I moved the furniture myself. The men complained, but I couldn't tell them what their boss told me about the drawers.

At least the little crowbar didn't have much stuff to move from her apartment. Roger Rockenbaugh helped me move Debi to our house on Whippoorwill Dr. I have learned to like our present house. It has surrounding trees, but isn't thirty acres of woods like Spring Falls or two hundred acres of woods like Rock River Farm. It is a great place to be right now as long as I am with Debi.

Of course, Jenny has passed now. I would have probably moved from her place by now anyway. That place is not the same now that Jenny and Bill Hays are gone. Cherokee is yet alive, but about the only person or thing left.

At least we got to visit him last winter, but he wasn't looking so well. You said he had cancer. He probably won't last much longer. He didn't look good.

I usually turned right instead of left coming out of the driveway when living at Jenny's place, that way avoided looking at the my old place. There were a few times when I did turn left and once saw you playing in the front yard. I doubt that you ever saw me pass by.

Oh, I'm getting melancholy about living close to you, but not being able to walk across the road to visit. It is difficult driving by the big white house even these days and remembering those times with you and Kaitlyn. I also remember the short time when you were yet there without Kaitlyn. I remember too well all that work making it a potential home place.

Sincerely,

Dad

CHAPTER V

Good-bye Saying

Dear Angela – *Contact*

I believe that I have not shared my experiences concerning Kaitlyn's spirit with anyone except Debi and am sure I have not shared them with you. I don't know what you believe concerning spirits or ghosts, but I will share my experiences with you anyway.

I believe that I had contact with the spiritual world through Kaitlyn. I woke up during the third night after Kaitlyn died. It was right after the funeral, I think. I am just not sure what night. I had a constant terrible pain in my chest since that day at the hospital when learning of Kaitlyn's death. It was as if someone had literally stabbed me in the chest with a huge knife. I physically ached all over anyway, but this was bad pain, right in the heart. I literally had a broken heart, a wounded heart, a ripped and torn heart.

Your mother was awake, lying in bed next to me, when she saw a misty, almost cloud-like figure hovering above me. I'm not sure what time it was during the night, but I was asleep. She told me about it later and that it disappeared when she noticed it.

I later woke and instantly saw something fly across the room away from me, something like a light or a white cloud. At the same time I heard a loud sound that awakened your mother.

She asked, "What was that?"

I couldn't answer that question. I said nothing. It was as if something had crashed against a window or an outside wall. I expected to see a big hole in the wall or at least a broken window. I got out of bed and walked to the unharmed wall. No damage in any way was present. I then realized that the pain in my chest was gone. It had left when that crash took place. It all happened fast and was surreal. The light cloud object that flew across the room and went through the wall apparently took the pain with it. I believe that it was Kaitlyn taking the pain away. I believe it was Kaitlyn in her natural spiritual body, hovering above and then flying away. It all sounds crazy I know, but I can only write about what I saw and felt.

I also believe that she took some long residing spirits with her when she left. I believe that there were Indian spirits present in our farmhouse. I heard them downstairs infrequently at night. They talked and made noises. Of course I couldn't understand what they were saying, but I mutely heard them as if a radio was on downstairs except there was no radio downstairs. They moved around, but did not harm anything or anybody. I learned to accept them.

I once had a man stop by our house asking me if I knew anything about its history. He said his ancestors once lived there. They were Indians and had picked out that particular spot because it was near the creek, shielded from cold winter winds by the gradual hill and remained cool during summer because of all the trees.

Of course the house was not there at that time, but it was indeed shielded from the cold wind and remained cool during the summer with little air conditioning. Construction of the original house was in 1846, the huge porch was added in 1920 and the addition was constructed about 1965. The original house floor joists were logs placed on huge rocks serving as a foundation. Someone put a modern concrete block foundation and 2" x 10" floor joists under it sometime during the past fifty years. Someone had kept two of the original stones visible.

It had gravel beneath the black top soil for good drainage. The fertile soil would grow almost anything. I had a garden below the bog. The garden never required more water than the basement spring provided via the bog. There was always slow steady seeping water for the garden. It grew great vegetables. Remember that slimy asparagus you planted and ate. It was big by the time we all moved.

I think the spring was surely there and used by the Indians before there was a basement. It must have been a great little Indian settlement. It was a great place for us. That house had a perfect setting. People commented about that house. I know the man who owned it before us surely didn't want to give it back to the bank. I think he had great plans for the place, little money and no incentive to work.

My friend Ron Keeling from Union Federal Bank finally foreclosed on the place. It included forty acres of mostly wooded land. He told me two years earlier that it might be available, and finally called one day, asking if I wanted it. I took a check with me. I knew it was perfect for me when I first stepped inside. It needed every kind of materials, fixtures, remodeling and TLC. I was the perfect man for that place. I loved it.

The Indian gave me his name and address, saying, "If you ever want to sell the place, I'd be interested in buying it."

I lost the piece of paper and couldn't contact him when finally having to sell it because of the divorce. I wanted to keep it, but I couldn't afford the place. It was too nice for me. I don't think I ever told you that story.

You and your mother stayed there for a year or so until she met Terry and moved to Florida. Do you remember much about the place? Did you feel bad about leaving it? You never said anything, but then you were only five years old and didn't express yourself much at that time.

Sincerely,

Dad

Dear Angela – *Three Incidents*

I had three more incidents that I believe were Kaitlyn communicating with me. I'm not quite sure why, but I accept my experiences in full faith.

I was sitting in the family room watching TV when I heard a rumbling sound. I first thought it was the TV. I ignored it, thinking it background noise. I heard it repeatedly. I finally muted the TV to listen closely. The sound was coming from what I thought was one side of the atrium doors. I got up, walked to the door, turned the knob and the door opened. It was unlocked. We never used those doors and certainly never left them unlocked. I then literally saw the doorknob vibrate, and totally believed that it was Kaitlyn telling me that the door was unlocked and to lock it. I locked it, returning to my chair, but I didn't turn the sound back on and the noise didn't occur again. I thought for a long time and then prayed a thank you prayer.

Another incident was when standing near Kaitlyn's oak ash box sitting on my chest of drawers, and I heard book pages turning. The sound was loud, not like normal pages turning, but loud enough that I could hear them from the next room, my bedroom. I finally walked into your bedroom and saw one of your favorite books lying open on the bed. Maybe someone had left it there from another day, or maybe, Kaitlyn was looking at it. There was no one in the room. The book was open. I can't explain how turning pages could have made so much noise. I have only one explanation, Kaitlyn.

Another time I was standing near her oak box. I rubbed it nearly every day and had worn a smooth place on it. It is yet smooth and I still touch it once in awhile. I heard the sound of flapping wings in my left ear. I could feel the air passing over my ear. I imagined a huge butterfly a half inch or so away from my ear, but I saw nothing. I believed it was Kaitlyn as an angel. It lasted for about ten seconds. I yet didn't see anything, but knew in my heart that it was Kaitlyn leaving this earth and saying good-bye. I didn't want to believe it, but knew I would never have another earthly contact with her.

She had stayed around long enough. I had my own witness to her heavenly assent. I asked for more, but never got more visits. I wonder how many incidents you had, Angela.

The best advice I can give someone who has lost a family member or friend is, "Keep your mind and heart open for contact." That is what I did and I was not disappointed. Oh God, I want more.

Sincerely,

Dad

Quiet Child

Child be quiet.
Sunlight smiles in your eyes.
Clever thoughts will meet you
When clocks watch and
Calendar months don't get torn.
Oh sweet child hear music
Where Mother sits and
Father doesn't go.

Your sister is glory gone.
Brother lives too far away.
Family matters fade, but
I feel sad for you anyway.
I can't help you grow because
I'm in between now and then.
Can you feel my tears
When I walk another way?

Oh sweet flower bloom with
Bright and right eyes.
I promise to teach
If chance gives and
I learn to not weep frequently.
So be quiet and
Listen to sluggish time.
You are sunlight growing nearer.

Correct Ears to Listen

In her silence
I feel what is
brewing in her mind;
truly in her mind, for
words distract and
tell only half truths.

Words too often are for
gaining attention and hiding
deep residing thoughts;
often they cause noise to
distract loneliness and
not feel isolation.

Her death relates to
her silence, but
when she finally speaks,
it will be after great thought,
idea consummation and
spiritual confirmation.

Indeed I'd love to
hear her speak and
know her mind,
but I can wait
until time is right and
I have correct ears to listen.

Dear Angela – *Drifting Apart*

It was the time immediately after Kaitlyn's passing that your mother and I drifted apart. It seemed to start when all of her family came up to Crawfordsville for the funeral. They were sympathetic with me while they were here. They were on our side concerning Kaitlyn, but after they left, things changed for some reason. Your mother and her family were estranging themselves before Kaitlyn's passing. They barely talked with us and your mother said she never wanted to be like them. I never understood what dynamic was taking place. I later reasoned that your mother only wanted to be with me in order to get away from them.

She later said in a psychological test, "I never loved Phil."

I thought she loved me, at least in the beginning. I guess she used me.

They all became close and grew to be against me after Kaitlyn passed. I don't know what she was telling them about me as I became the enemy. I witnessed this about the Giffins before, concerning other people. It seemed people were either friend or foe to them. I became foe. I never understood why I became the enemy.

Sometimes I think your mother thought I blamed her for Kaitlyn's death, but I never said anything. Maybe it was because I possibly thought it. I think to this day that some of your and Kaitlyn's problems were due to your mother's earlier bad habits. I'm talking about drugs and alcohol, especially when she was a teenager. We discussed this before she ever got pregnant. She told me that she discussed the possibility of being gene and chromosome damaged with the doctors at the Indiana University Medical Center.

I didn't want to chance creating a child with foreseen problems. I wanted to avoid bringing a child into the world with predisposed hindrances or disadvantages. I never had a problem loving a child who might naturally come into my life with physical or mental problems. Maybe I shouldn't have thought that way. Maybe I shouldn't be airing my mind with you now. Forgive me if I say things that you don't want to hear or wish not to believe.

Anyway, your mother and I drifted apart, she grieved in her way and I in mine. I had the Holy Spirit as my counselor. I'm not sure who she had as a therapist, but I think she surely needed one.

I pray nearly every day that the Holy Spirit is with you. We both always need Him.

Sincerely,

Dad

Dear Angela – *Like an Angel*

I am sure you don't remember or didn't even know at the time, about my struggle at school and at home after Kaitlyn died. You had your own personal struggle. I wish I had been more attentive to your needs. I thought I was attentive, but later realized that I wasn't thoughtful enough. I lost my enthusiasm for family, work and life in general. I rededicated my life to you, but that wasn't enough to get me over the despair and misery.

It was during the spring of 1997 or the next year after Kaitlyn passed that I needed to learn how to operate a Computerized Numerical Control lathe at school. I found a man named Chris Rowland, who I mentioned earlier, that worked at California Pellet Mill. He was the lead engineer in charge of programming at CPM. He volunteered to help me several Saturdays, teaching me how to program and operate the lathe. He also helped with the CNC milling machine, teaching me more about programming and machining.

A teacher in my area of Industrial Technology had retired and I inherited the metal machining classes and laboratory. I needed to re-educate myself concerning several machines and learn about some new machines.

Chris taught me about the machines and I learned how to program and operate them. I was then able to teach my students. He introduced me to a completely new area of education. He took the time to encourage and instill interest in computers, automation and machining. He was like an angel sharing new knowledge and enthusiasm. It partially took my mind off Kaitlyn's death. I gained a new passion for living, learning and education. I owe Chris Rowland a great deal. I don't know if I ever told him about my loss at that time or not. I thanked him, but not enough.

I called him the other day, after all these years, and thanked him again for his help. Writing these letters jogged my memory of him and brought back my gratitude. I told him over the phone about appearing at the right time and being like a helping angel. He also assisted in mending my broken heart.

Later that year a man from Eli Lily came along and donated some obsolete Zymark Robots to the school. He asked if I wanted some junk. They were not obsolete or junk to me, but were priceless to my pre-engineering program. My superintendant flew me out to Worchester, Massachusetts twice and put me up in a hotel for the three-day classes to learn about programming and operating the robots. A man at Zymark said if I could get out there, he would let me take the classes free. My superintendant also paid a technician to come to my school and trouble shoot why the robots wouldn't allow new or edited programming. The tech found one small file that needed to be loaded for them to work properly. It was a safety/ security file. Once it was loaded, I was in business. You saw the robots operate, didn't you?

So you see there were several angels helping me to get my life back in order, but Chris got it all started. He was the main angel at work in my life, but I think the Holy Spirit was overseeing the whole operation.

I believe that I later served as an angel myself in Herman, Missouri. I think God uses us occasionally as angels or angels use our bodies. I was not myself and was bold and truthful concerning faith. I spoke like a preacher, not a schoolteacher.

I had stopped at Herman a few times before when going out west to visit Kristen. Angela, we stopped there at least once I know. Do you remember Herman? It was that little German town on the Missouri River with all the small wineries and that one big winery named Stone Hill. We took a tour of Stone Hill. Herman is where I get that great *Hunter's Red* wine from the Adam Puchta Winery. I know, you don't drink wine. I think you have been to the Adam Puchta Winery.

Anyway, I was compelled to drive down by the far end of the Herman River Park. I parked my truck near a bench where a man sat by himself. I was compelled to walk near him. I was compelled to say hello.

I asked, "How's it going?"

"Not good," he answered.

"Do you want to talk?" I don't know why I asked that question. I was not interested in hearing about someone's problems. I stood behind the bench while he sipped from a bottle in a paper bag.

He started talking about how he lost his wife six months ago from an electrical accident, how he lost his two kids to the courts because of his drinking and how he needed back surgery. He went on to say that when they X-rayed him before the surgery, they found cancer. They didn't operate, but instead put him on chemotherapy and gave him a 40% chance to live. He was there by the river debating whether to take his life or not. He said that I came along just in time, and that he was about to walk into the river.

I listened for nearly an hour and finally started talking with him about the situation. As I said, I spoke like a preacher, like an angel I think. I had answers for him that I didn't know I had in me. I spoke wise words. I gave spiritual guidance.

I asked, "Do you believe in Jesus?"

He answered, " Yes."

I don't know how I had the courage to ask that question. Like I said, I was not myself. I felt like an angel giving advice. My final advice was to take a chance on the 40% even though the odds weren't the best.

I said, "You never know, maybe a miracle might happen. You have had enough bad luck; it's time for some good luck. Why not take a chance. Hey, 40% is better than 0%. I say go for beating the odds."

I placed my hand on his shoulder. "I say forget the river, take a chance on God."

He turned towards me with tears in his eyes and thanked me repeatedly. "You're like an angel," he whispered. "Are you an angel?"

"No, I'm just a man like you who knows what hard times are like."

I turned away from him, got in my truck and drove away. I saw him yet sitting on the bench as I turned onto the highway. A blazing red dusk sky in my rearview mirror filled my eyes. It reminded of my smallness and unimportance, and yet I felt somewhat worthy. I also felt a little embarrassed for my behavior, but a little holy at the same time. Angel remnants were stuck in my mind. I still felt a little bit like an angel. "Forgive my arrogance," I whispered.

I wonder if you have ever felt the influence of an angel. I think Kaitlyn is sometimes an angel, looking over others in need. I think she is your guardian angel. I wonder how many times angels are active in our lives. I wonder how many people have felt like an angel for a short time period. Maybe I wonder too much. Maybe signs and miracles aren't real. I wonder.

Sincerely,

Dad

Dear Angela – *Playmate*

Your friend Emma came to play one day. She was coming through the house from the front door as I walked towards the family room looking for you. I glanced through the pass-through between the kitchen and family room before I reached the doorway. It was easy to see everything and everyone in the family room from that vantage point. You were in the center of the room laughing and playing seemingly with someone, but you were alone. I called your name and told you about Emma. You immediately turned and saw me looking through the pass-through.

You then turned back to the original direction and away from me and said, "I have to go now," and with a serious look said, "Good-bye."

You then changed your facial expression from serious to happy and headed for the front room where Emma waited. I had seen that same action and concentration once before. I saw it when you were seemingly gazing and speaking to someone else not there, but I thought nothing of it. This took place, of course, before I left the house due to the divorce.

You rushed towards the front living room with a big smile. I believe you never invited Emma to play with your other playmate. I also believe that playmate was Kaitlyn. I once talked to Laurie Hatcher, Emma's mother, about you pretending that Kaitlyn was a playmate. I don't know how the subject came up, but she thought it was more than pretending. She believed that Kaitlyn was present. She saw you acting the same way one time herself as if playing with Kaitlyn.

Laurie and your mother used to be good friends, but something happened between them and your mother cut off the relationship. Laurie said she never knew what happened. Why your mother wanted nothing to do with her all of a sudden was a mystery. Your mother never let you see Emma anymore after her falling out with Laurie. I think a great friendship was lost. Emma was my favorite of your friends, except for Kaitlyn, of course. Can you tell me more about that? I tried to get you girls together at least once during your summer visits after moving to Florida.

Remember that time I took you and Emma to the Indianapolis Zoo? I felt really privileged and honored that Laurie trusted me enough to let me take her precious little daughter to the zoo.

My heart tells me that you played with Kaitlyn on and off for several months after her passing. My intellect tells me that it was all in our minds. Only you can answer that question. That is if you can remember. I surely do remember.

Sincerely,

Dad

Seeking As One

You never have to carry a
heavy load alone, for in
your life reside those
who can help,
lift and pull,
hoist and control that which
seems too burdensome.

In your eyes
I see sadness of which
you will not share.
And, on this day,
sitting among us,
you are far away in
thought and emotion.

Let me know your
weaknesses and strengths,
your suspicions and worries.
Our lives are intertwined like
daily created music and
held together with love of
each other's song.

Dear Angela – *Shared Grief*

I don't want to relive the time when Kaitlyn passed, but I would like to go back and comfort you more. It was so much a blur that I don't remember being with you enough. I should have comforted you more. I shouldn't have grieved inside so much, but shared our grief. I wish I had held and talked with you more.

We can never go back. We can only wish we could go back. Well, if we could go back, knowing what I know now, things would be much different. Then again, I'm not sure I could have changed anything that happened. God's plan is God's plan.

I do regret one thing. I wish I had prayed more. I wish I had read the signs better and prayed more. I wish I had been able to see the future just a little bit. I wish I had known the Holy Spirit better then, and as I do now.

I yet wish to know Him better every day. I feel so inadequate most of the time. I wish I could be aware of the spiritual world more. It is right in front of my face and I can't see it. It is as near as my soul, mind and spirit, but I cannot truly locate it.

I think my soul is near the center of my body, some place near my belly button. I think my mind is in my head some place. I think my spirit is in every cell of my body. I wish I could touch any one of them. Yet, I sit here ignorant and weak, seeking that which is untouchable, silent and covert. It's strange how something so illusive can have such a bearing on one's life.

Sincerely,

Dad

Fermenting Life

I measure gathering days with
mixed lament, sometimes wishing
tomorrow had never come,
thinking time is no friend of mine.
With aging body I write, speak, and
learn less, but forget more.
Future seeks my attention, but
past haunts and makes me pray.

Yet in calm mood I hum
melodies long ago learned and
quietly recite love poems
expressed in forgotten ways.
In places where roses bloom
year round and rain washes minds,
there are ageless moments seeping
today that I will never regret.

I find age, time and
seasons faltering in rolling hill
vineyards, where I pick
sweet grapes and ferment them
well into what makes me drunk.
I find joy in time spent
between yesterday's
passing and tomorrow's arrival.

Dear Angela – *Divorce*

There are many reasons and ways to say good-bye, and we have experienced several. One more happened about a year after Kaitlyn passed to heaven. It was when we had planned to visit Kristen in Colorado, but your mother decided not to come and wanted you to stay home with her.

Your mother and I had touched each other but one time, and that was a hard-lipped kiss, after Kaitlyn passed. We shared no physical romantic contact. Your mother wanted a substitute for Kaitlyn. I just wanted to deal with the black hole left in our lives from her passing. She considered many ways of filling the loss of your sister, including adopting five Russian boys. I don't know where that came from, but to say the least, I was worried about your mother's state of mind.

She is a physically, mentally and emotionally tough woman. Maybe it's that Scottish blood in her. Sometimes I think you are much like her in that way. For me, I am tough physically and mentally, but weak emotionally.

What worried me most was that she never blamed herself for Kaitlyn's death. I was afraid that she would think that immediately after her passing, but it never happened. I think it would have been natural for her to blame herself, and then when she did, everyone would assure her that it was not her fault. I thought that after her teenage history and early adulthood background with alcohol and drugs, that she would feel some possible guilt.

I insisted that they test her before getting pregnant in the first place. She beat me over the head with the idea of having children for at least a year. I finally consented to take part in having children.

I really didn't want more children, but when I saw that ultrasound of you and Kaitlyn, I realized that you girls were the greatest blessing in my life. You gave renewed purpose and meaning to my life. I then and there dedicated the rest of my life to you girls. I later then found myself with only one of you. I rededicated my life to you, Angela, the rest of my life.

It was a tough time because everyone was going nowhere in his or her own way. There was a big black hole in our family. Filling it was impossible, at least I thought so, but your mother sought a substitute.

Of course, I can't say that with much conviction because I can only judge her mental state by her actions. She seemed like a desperate woman, searching for help and I was not part of the solution.

Anyway, when I reached Kristen's house I didn't know what was going on in Crawfordsville. I found out when I got there that your mother had called Kristen and said she was filing for divorce. She was going to Cleveland to be with a friend and was of course taking you with her.

I was shocked because she had given me a big hug just before I left. I was thinking that things were about to change, that she was soul searching and allowing me to be part of her solution. I misread that hug. It turned out to be something akin to the Mafia kiss of death. Things got very complicated from that time on.

Your mother talked to Kristen on the phone before I got there and told her that I was suicidal, and that she took my handgun. Kristen got up in the middle of the night crying, asking me about what your mother had said.

Kristen said, "Aaron and I have been watching you and saw no signs of suicidal tendencies."

I reassured Kristen that it was not remotely possible. Your mother later said she had been worried about me for some time.

Then I ask, "Why didn't she take the handgun sooner and also the shotgun?" I don't think she was too worried about me. I think she was planning her leaving me for more than a year. I found out in retrospect that she had been stealing money from our lockbox and bank account. She had been using charge cards without my knowledge. I think she was deviously planning her get-a-way. I was stupid.

The exact opposite was true about me, especially by the time I arrived at Kristen's house. I had just experienced a spiritual journey. I traveled down through Branson, Missouri and camped at a place called *The Angels Campground*.

I felt directed to Sam Butcher's *Precious Moments Chapel*. People call it "America's Sistine Chapel." It has over 9,000 square feet of Butcher's original biblical artwork on the walls and ceilings. I walked through the gardens after visiting the chapel and stopped at a special prayer room for those who have lost a child. Butcher had experienced the worst himself. It was a moving experience and a remarkable place.

I drove through the panhandle of Texas. I saw a giant cross probably twenty miles away and approached it with interest. It was located at the small town of Groom, Texas. I drove by it, but kept looking at it. I was compelled to turn around and investigate the place. It was the reason for the founding of the *Cross of Our Lord Jesus Christ Ministries*. God apparently put Steve Thomas and his wife in charge of building the cross and they got the job done.

They say a 1,000 people stop to see the cross every day. It's 19 stories tall. There is also a circle of stations of sculpted statues created by a man named Mickey Wells. The likeness statues depict Christ's final ordeal. They are life size bronze statues from Pilate's decision to crucify Jesus to the crucifixion itself. One station shows Christ falling for the first time as he was carrying the cross. I literally looked into His eyes through the sculpted likeness. It moved me very much. The whole experience changed me. I stayed there for several hours. I left a different person.

I then drove through New Mexico taking a two-lane road from Tucumcari to Los Vegas, New Mexico. I stopped to hear the silence of the desert. It seemed like nothing lived out there, not even rodents. It seemed like I heard the whispering of the Holy Spirit as I looked out over the flat land from a high mountain perch. I was very much alone except that I felt I was in God's House and Kaitlyn was with me.

The whole trip seemed a preparation for what I was about to hear. I was full of the Holy Spirit by the time I got to Denver.

The bad news was not so bad. In fact, you know as well as I do that when you have suffered the worst, everything else is not so bad. The news I received from your mother, deep down inside, didn't bother me so much. Actually, it was the best thing your mother could do for me. We were both better off apart, but I sincerely don't believe that it was best for you. Sorry.

My lawyer later told me that what your mother did was the same as all of John Capper's clients. Capper was a scumbag lawyer and I think many people would agree with me. I think he isn't very smart and had only one game plan, and he used it every time in divorce court. He had a reputation of being good at his job. I don't know what he is like these days. I bet he is still using the same divorce game plan.

He instructs, or at least he used to tell all of his clients to leave town, go to a friend's house, accuse the husband of suicidal tendencies and paint him as a possible violent man.

During that time Freckles got sick, and finally got maggots in her butt. I took her to the vet and they treated her and told me what to do for her. I did treat her for several days, but was unable to help her. I finally contacted your mother, telling her that Freckles was dying and that she needed to come home if she wanted to say good-bye to her. I said my good-byes before you and your mother returned. Freckles held out until you and your mother returned. We took Freckles to the vet and she died on the way.

It was a time when I also had to say good-bye to my wife, home, way of life and partially good-bye to you. I got divorce papers served on me and as I read them, I thought the terrible things stated in the papers were not about me, but actually about your mother. Medication was required, said the papers, and that suicidal tendencies were present and counseling was needed. I thought she was the one on the edge, falling apart and mentally ill, but the accusations were about me. I realized it once I sorted out the legal lingo.

Your mother later tried buying me off, wanting me to never see you again. She offered me $30,000. I didn't know where she was going to get the money, from her dad I guessed. She was too greedy to offer at least the farm. I was shocked at her attitude. I'm your father, will always be your father and you will never have someone to take my place. I will never truly say good-bye to you. No amount of money could have turned me away from you. It was the first of many attempts to take you away from me. I never understood why she wanted to destroy the love between us. You needed my influence. I needed to give you attention and love. I understood that love destruction agenda less the more she tried to pull us apart. I am yet confused about her behavior.

I know it was difficult for you, trying to balance your attention and not show your affection when the other parent was around. I hope all the tension and anxiety did not damage you in any way. I hope that is not something that helped cause your final action to estrange us.

I don't blame you for your actions. I only pray for your reconciliation of the situation. The truth will surely win out. I think you need some precious moments inspiration or some Groom, Texas visiting.

Sincerely,

Dad

Reds, Yellows and Purples

On petals light
like wind itself,
collected moisture
burns off in
appreciating
sunlight on a
September morning.
Gallant
protective leaves
shutter with
glee for in
sun's coming,
another day is
born.
Bright reds,
yellows and
purples paint an
eastern sky.
For millions of
years such
beauty
faithfully has
gathered,
screaming for
attention through a
tree canopy.
And yet,
dew soaked
petals and
green leaves
turning yellow,
I mostly notice while
recording eyes
gaze downward on
wondrous

leaf swept path.
Warm sun
rises higher,
seeking some pinnacle
later in day and
then begins
its slow western
earth fall,
trying to
repeat morning's
glorious artful
design.
Reds, yellows and
purples
it seems are
most striking.
Seeing and
appreciating them
consumes most of
my morning.
I then step from
thick forest into a
green grassy field and
full sunlight bakes
my September skin.
Too soon due
will be snow, and
warm sun
will be cold cloud hidden.
Too soon those reds,
yellows and purples
will be gray.
Too soon
my canopy
will be naked.
Too soon I
will not remember
walking here.

Dear Angela – *Parental Alienation*

I don't know if you are or were ever aware that your mother continually tried to keep us apart; from the day she tried to bribe me until today I suspect. I believe that she has nearly succeeded. Our future depends on you. You are almost 18 years old. You are old enough to make most of your own decisions. Your mother has been on a program of Parental Alienation for a long time. We even discussed it at hearings in front of the judge twice. I have never understood her motives.

During our first summer together when I lived at Jenny's and after you had moved to Florida, your mother had several of her women friends call me nearly every day, asking for you to come and spend time with them. They called it a play date. I called it stealing our time. We didn't have that much visitation time and I finally asked them to quit harassing me with the phone calls. I would have considered it at first with a couple of them, but not after all the harassment. All of them did quit calling accept Cheryl Furman, a member of Christ Lutheran Church, a woman in good standing, a so called good Christian woman. People are not always what they seem. Remember that. Some days she called twice. She continued for many days even after my requesting our privacy. She finally gave up because I kept saying "no."

I had to fight for our together time, whether it was during the summer or during the week. I felt that you needed my influence and I need your company. I wished to show my love for you. That all changed when your mother met Terry and decided to move to Florida. I found out that you all were leaving for Florida before a hearing could take place concerning terms of visitation. I found out on Thursday that you, your mother and Terry were having a going away party on Friday night before the Monday hearing and that you all were leaving Saturday. Now that sounds complicated with all those days. Forgive my German need for detail.

I learned about your leaving in time to talk to Bill Hays who was a lawyer besides being a writer and businessperson. Do you remember Bill, Jenny's husband? I told him my discovery and he told me to get an injunction, preventing your mother from taking you away. He was a little man, as you probably remember, but he was tough.

He pounded on his kitchen table while saying,
"Get an injunction, get an injunction."

I had to pound on my lawyer's office table the next day while saying, "Get an injunction, get an injunction."

He finally agreed to get the injunction and later said that he didn't think your mother would do such a thing. She wanted all hearings concerning you to take place in Florida instead of Indiana. I foiled her alienation program. We got the injunction on Friday, the day of the party.

The judge told your mother, "You can go to Florida, but the child stays here until we work out the visitation arrangements."

I know your mother and Terry were upset with me, but I had to fight for our time together. My lawyer, Jim Bowlin, said that he misjudged your mother. He said that several times later when conflict surfaced and she tried to pull a trick on me. One time I remember when your mother was coming up to settle something having to do with your getting Social Security money. You get the money because I am sixty-five years old and you are a minor. There was to be a hearing, but the judge and the lawyers decided to work things out behind closed doors. Your mother had told me that there was no need for a hearing. However, when she and Terry came to pick you up from the summer visit, she informed me that she did indeed want a hearing.

After your mother arrived, you wanted nothing to do with Debi and me. You would not look at us when we arrived at the second floor of the courthouse. You had been happy and loving just the day before; then with your mother present, you were cold, sad and nervous. You didn't even acknowledge us when we stepped off the elevator. Debi approached and hugged you, but you didn't hug back. It was strange. We all went in a room and you waited outside. Your mother informed us then that she wanted the hearing.

She and Terry were angry and mentally blew up in front of my lawyer. It was like something out of a movie. They were talking about all kinds of things, visitation time with other children, less time with me, needing more money for insurance.

It was bizarre. I saw you in the hallway taking it all in. I couldn't judge how you felt about what was happening. Debi and I couldn't understand what caused all the anger. It was as if they had worked themselves into frenzy before arriving at the courthouse. Your mother claimed in court that you didn't want to spend time with me, that you cried and fretted about coming to Indiana. She finally claimed in court that she wanted more money for your health insurance and that the cost before the deductable limit was too much for them to handle. She also wanted us to have a shorter summer visit. The judge asked me a few questions. I only remember one of them and the answer I gave him.

I said, "Yes, I am selfish about our time together, and I don't want to share Angela much. I'm selfish because I think Angela needs me as much as I need her. I think she needs my influence."

The judge finally made a decision after taking you back to his chambers to talk. He came out and told me that I should pay more of the pre-deduction money, but he kept our visitation time at five weeks. That decision resulted in me paying some health cost, and most of your braces cost. I didn't mind. I think you will have an even more wonderful smile when the braces come off. I hope to see that smile when that day comes.

I've never been able to understand why your mother wished us apart. I gathered that she constantly wished me out of your life, out of her life. She treated me like *Uncle Phil*, rather than *Father Phil*. Maybe someday you'll be able to explain it to me, that is if you are aware of it and understand it yourself. I think your mother has done a lot of mental damage to you.

Sorry if I ramble and speak too boldly about your mother. I have a feeling that you know what I'm talking about even if I show prejudice and lop-sided thinking. I have especially noticed a distancing from you during the past couple of years. I don't know how or when your mother told you that I am not your biological father. I think you changed your relationship with me after that revelation. I hope you yet think of me as your father. I am your father.

There is no one in the world who can push my buttons like your mother. She thinks I am an angry person, but I'm not. I only talk with her when there are issues between us. She can really get me upset. I think you know that already.

I'm glad you'll soon be 18 years old and be a liberated woman. Wow, that seems impossible. We are truly time travelers.

Sincerely,

Dad

Equality

Equality sits beyond an
oak door, arms folded,
jaw set, waiting, waiting.
Men speak loudly
beyond that door,
beyond brass door handle,
like a locked stoic hand,
waiting, waiting.
No one knocks,
no one turns handle,
no one pushes against
its heavy resistance.
An old bench near door,
slick from sitting,
remains unashamed.
Everyone removes a
little dust every day and
keeps it clean.
Court is in session today.
Equality seeks answers in
morning light shining
through opaque window glass.
Sweat beads on grim faces.
Pain stirs in heavy hearts.
There is no dust on equality,
or in brassy hearts,
for equality is like that
oak courthouse door,
waiting, waiting to be
opened.

Dear Angela – *Time Together*

Let's talk a little bit about our time together before you moved to Florida, the time before I had to say good-bye except for summer and Christmas visits. I cherished those times, even though I wished for more because they were too few.

Do you remember how we went to the zoo, camping and biking? Do you remember eating at your favorite place, the Chinese restaurant downtown? Do you remember when we took our walks in the woods, when we collected all those wild flowers and when you learned how to drive the riding lawn mower? We hooked the mower up to the trailer and I rode in it while sitting on a lawn chair. You drove and I rode in the trailer on the forest path. I felt like some Jamaican sitting on a fringe-decorated buggy passing through town in a parade.

I will not go into much more. I just wanted to jolt your memory about our times together. We have so many great times to remember while living at Jenny's farmhouse. I remember when we decided to take care of Jenny's horses. She was looking for someone and was talking about some older girl taking care of them. I knew it wouldn't be fair for someone other than us, or more exactly you, taking care of them. I knew it would have to be us, even though I didn't really want to do it. You needed help with them, but thought you alone were taking care of them. It would have been depriving you of a great pleasure if someone else fed, rode and boarded them. You loved those horses, especially Cherokee. Cherokee was a special horse for sure. I think he is yet alive, but not doing so well.

Remember that time when he was showing off by running up and down the hills, and he stubbed his toe and nearly fell. He recovered from the near fall, seemingly embarrassed, but trying not show it. He remained cool, calm and collected as if nothing had happened. Almost as if he had planned it. He was a cool guy for sure. Of course, we tend to put human emotions to animal behavior. I'm sure they don't have our emotions. The last time we saw him was during the summer of 2009. I wonder if we will ever see him again.

It's sad that Dodger, Gartez and Bucky are all gone now. I guess many animals have already come and gone in your life. By animals having shorter lives than humans, many pass through our lives and it's hard to keep track of them all. We remember the humans very well. Can you imagine how many animals have passed through my life? Now I'm down to Kiddy Kidee. I wonder if I will ever have another animal besides Kidee. I know you'll have many many more.

Sincerely,

Dad

Dear Angela – *Cards*

I hope you kept all those cards I sent you. They'll make a great scrapbook some day for remembering your childhood. I sent you a card almost every week for years, at least eleven or twelve years, I bet. I collected all those stickers and filled the front of the envelope every week. I yet have many stickers. I guess I won't use them much anymore.

I thought they were great, but was always afraid that there were too many stickers and the post office machine wouldn't be able to read the address, and would be unable to recognize the address on the envelope. I think that maybe some of them didn't get there because of that problem. I never put many stickers on an envelope that contained money. I didn't want it to get lost. I usually asked if you got the ones with money and you always said yes.

I used to call you twice a week. I think many times you didn't want to be bothered, so you didn't pick up. I think your mother also knew and didn't pick up when I consistently called at 9:00 pm on Monday, Wednesday and Friday. I would rather think you were outside or busy. I guess you had caller ID. Oh well, that is behind us. I spoke to you at least once nearly every week. All I needed was to know that you were well and happy.

A few times, I didn't hear from you for a couple of weeks and I got worried. There was usually no reason for me to be worried. A couple of times you were on the road in Missouri. I wasn't so good at talking on the phone and you said you weren't either, but I needed to make contact frequently.

Just a short call and a quick "I love you," was all I needed.

One thing that always bothered me when I called and you didn't answer was your recorded message on the answering machine, "This is the Parns." That message was on there for years. I bet it is yet on the machine. I used to pull the phone away from my ear during that message. I guess it was the thing of you using the Parn name. I hope you will always be a Reisner.

I have noticed the last year or so that you have been using the name, Reisner-Parn, on your emails and Facebook. That bothers me quite a bit. I don't know whose idea that was, but it doesn't seem right. How can that be your legal name? I guess when you turn 18, you can use whatever name you wish.

Sincerely,

Dad

Mental Movies

You were a
precious flower
I couldn't hold, for
time was
not our friend.

You were taken from
me too soon,
physically,
mentally and
emotionally.

I had only a
little part in
another's grand plan.
There was little
space for me.

And you with
your will to be
fair and patient,
grew as any flower
wishing to be free.

I was left with
tools quietly laying on
shelves made for
carpenters,
not gardeners.

I strived for
liberty myself and
left no
reluctant tool untouched or
willing love unfelt.

Summer came and
you were with me.
I cherished your roots,
stalk and bloom.
I was truly grateful.

I held you infrequently,
I always had a
gardener's desire,
film-maker's skill and a
father's love.

Dear Angela – *Wild About Horses*

Do you remember that hot summer day after moving to Georgia when we picked you up at your house? You rode your horse in the ring. I was impressed. There was also that time when I watched you during a lesson. I was impressed then also. You rode well and consistently got better.

I later watched you during summer horse camp at Wild About Horses here in Lafayette. Debi and I went to the show at Delphi and you did really well, except when the saddle slipped and you went over the horse's head. Hey, you didn't fall off. That was good.

You really liked it down at WAH with Pam Bowen. She does a great job working with her students. I thought you would have a place like that some day. Maybe you will, who knows?

I often think about what you will finally do in life, what will be your vocation or profession. You have a lot of attributes, but loving and taking care of animals is one of your strongest. You used to say veterinarian medicine was for you. Remember when we took that tour of the School of Veterinarian Medicine at Purdue. We were hoping you would come to Lafayette, live with us and go to Purdue. You could yet, you know. You could have free room and board, and half tuition. You have only four more years to take advantage of the half tuition because Debi will teach only four more years at Purdue. I would love it if you came here and lived with us during college, but I guess you would have to give up your horses for nine months and that would be tough because you are "wild about horses."

I hope you remember how well you and Debi got along from the very first time meeting. You were pals. We had a great time all together going to Michigan on our trip during the summer of 2008.

Our New York trip the next summer was also great fun while staying in the travel trailer. Do you remember when I drove the Watkins Glen racetrack? You wanted to drive a lap, but I didn't want to share. Sorry. If you remember, you also didn't have a license to drive. There are so many great summer experiences to remember.

We also had great Christmas visits. I sure will miss spending that kind of time with you and Debi. You usually helped put up our tree. I remember one year you and Debi put all the decorations on it, but only after you wore them around while dancing to some crazy Christmas music. I think I have some pictures of that somewhere. I have that silly picture when you decorated me. We put up the tree again this year, but it wasn't the same without you.

I yet have some childish ways and my imagination will not quit, but it takes a lot of faith to think that tomorrow will be better. It's like believing that black ominous clouds do have renewing rain and on their edges exists sunlight enough for rainbows.

I guess all our craziness will end now that you will soon be eighteen and a liberated woman. We love you very much. I hope you realize that fact and will yet allow us in your life.

Sincerely,

Dad

Cold Rain

Cold rain beats
fresh spring leaves.
Nature is rhythmically
speaking with
drumming,
thumping and
growling.
She's dropping
rain droplets from
dark ominous
island clouds.
I can nearly
hear laughter
among surrounding
forest trees as
they accept
Nature's gift.
Sun then signals
storm's calm
retreat and
filters light into
my seeking
imagination, a
rainbow of
curved colors in
arching grace.
A gold filled pot
waits discovery.
I childishly
seek magic, as a
faith advocate, and
ignorantly decide
my hopeful fate.
I march towards an
ever moving

rainbow and
locate its
beginning place.
I'm disappointed for
merely soft
earth waits
my discovery.
Imagination yet
leisurely wanders.
Faith yet
remains strong.
My childish
ways will not
pass as
I stand in
Nature's gleaming
warm sun,
empty handed, yet
rainbow hopeful.

CHAPTER VI

Bridge Burning

Dear Angela – *Bad News*

It's hard to believe that the last time I saw you was after Christmas of 2009. We dropped you off after New Years of 2010. Your mother met us where her brother Brad lives in Georgia. We spent that Christmas vacation in the travel trailer at Carrabelle. That didn't work out so well. It was just too small and tight. We sold it the next summer. Now we're in a condominium and it's much better. I think you stayed with us five days during the three weeks in Florida. That seems so long ago.

The last time I talked with you was when you called me in June saying that you were going to Jacksonville for a three-week medical visit. I remember you telling me about how you were having more problems with the condromas, that you were having a lot of arthritis pain and that you were having some nerve damage problems. I was miserable hearing you say all those things were happening. I was aware of the condromas and arthritis, but not the nerve damage. I also didn't want to admit that your health was getting worse. I felt helpless, not being able to aid and comfort you.

You said you were going down to a clinic where there were great doctors that could help you. You said that they had seen all three conditions before, but not in one person.

I remember you saying something else to me. You started crying and said, "That's not the worst of it."

I was scared. I thought what could be more awful than all those health problems. I thought bad times were heading your way or something terrible had beset you. My worst fear was that you only had a few years to live or something like that. I was sad, afraid and anxious, but I patiently waited for you to continue. I was scared to hear the truth.

You finally told me, "The worst is that I can't come up to see you this July and August because the trip to Jacksonville is during that time."

I remember what a relief it was to know the worst was not bad at all.

I told you "Don't worry about the visit. Take care of yourself first. That's the most important thing."

You then stopped crying. We talked more and you said, "I love you, Dad," before hanging up.

All I have ever wanted was for you to be happy, healthy and alive. All I really needed, and need now, is to know that you are alive. I already lost Kaitlyn to Jesus. I don't want to lose you to anyone or anything on Earth.

"Please God watch over Angela," I pray every day.

I was yet worried about you, but not quite as much. I didn't feel sorry for myself because of the non-visit situation. I could only feel sorrow for you. I hardly ever feel sorry for myself anyway, now that I think about it. I'm not saying that I don't sometimes feel a little sorry for myself. I just think it's easier feeling sorry for others. I always look for the easy way out. It is easier thinking about others. It gets complicated thinking about one's selfish wants and needs.

I usually blame myself when things go wrong, then realize that it's a blessing and back off. It's a pattern of mine: something goes wrong, usually due to my stupidity, I then get upset with myself and then realize things are what they are. I finally realize the situation is small and not serious and then usually laugh at myself. It's that simple most of the time. Ok, sometimes bad things do happen and it's not easy to discard reality, and sometimes it's not my fault. It seems occasionally that bad luck just accumulates.

I think sometimes God allows the devil to play games with me. I just laugh when finally realizing apparent truth. It slowly seeps from my subconscious as reality teaches. All I can do is laugh. I wonder if I will be able to laugh when on my accruing weakness deathbed; when one thing goes wrong, then another and then another until fading like a sun caused breeze. God, I hope so. I hope I get the chance to drift away while whispering good-bye.

Sincerely,

Dad

Our Bridges

How can one
strike a match to
burn a bridge with a
clear conscience?
In a moment's
missspeak, a
relationship
can be
damaged,
sometimes
beyond repair, like a
match to tinder.

In my heart
I sense
something
very complicated,
something
very wrong that a
match can't fix.
Bridges are
seldom repaired or
rebuilt like
original structure and
beauty.

How then might
I save our bridge?
How might
I repair
damage done
except to remain
afar with
no words or
actions to redeem
hurtful words?
I am innocent.
God knows for sure.

I could never
hurt or
damage someone
I so admire.
I am only a worrier
when need be.
I am always
willing and
able to extinguish and
help repair a
bridge that
bears our name.

Dear Angela – *Shocked*

It was on June 15 that I noticed a note and a business card on my front door. I had been to Evansville concerning my truck transmission and had not been home for several days. We seldom use the front door so Debi didn't notice it either. It had been there for a couple of days. Well, I looked at it carefully and was perplexed about what it might concern. The business card was from a Justin Dearinger of the Indiana Department of Child Services. There was no indication to what it related. All it said was that we needed to talk. I called Mr. Dearinger immediately. He told me that it had to do with you. I was further perplexed.

"What's it about?" I asked.

He said that he couldn't discuss it over the phone and that I needed to come to the DCS office. Well, all kinds of thoughts flitted through my head. The first idea was that you had finally had enough of what was going in Georgia and wanted to come to live with us. I guess that was just hopeful thinking. Anyway, I saw on the card that he was also an investigator in financial aid matters. I then thought it was probably about getting more money after the Social Security runs out because you're going to college. I couldn't think of any other reason that he would need to speak with me.

I made an appointment and went downtown to see him the next day. He was a young man, wearing a T-shirt and frayed jeans. He didn't look very professional, but at that time I didn't know what his profession was anyway. We sat down in a private room. He started asking personal questions. You know things like age, occupation and marital status. I answered a few questions, and then asked what my being there concerned.

He said, "I can't say right now. Please answer the questions."

I answered a few more questions and finally asked again, "Why am I here?"

He didn't want to say at that time, but did go ahead and mention that it concerned you. He then continued to say that it had to do with allegations of physical abuse. I looked down at the folder with your name on it. I saw Angela Reisner-Parn on the heading. I got a bit upset about the name.

I asked, "What is the name on that folder?"

He replied, "Angela Reisner-Parn."

I told him that I had been down this road before, and that your mother had tried to use the name Parn before in several different ways.

"Parn is not her name," I said brashly.

I explained that I had once tracked down your school after dropping you off during a Christmas visit. I don't think I ever told you about this. For some reason when I was taking you back to your house, we came near your school. I knew we were close to the school because you had mentioned once that it was near your house. It was as if you saw the school or indicated by your attitude that we were close to it. I rather read your reaction when I asked where it was located. It was as if you didn't want me to know where it was located or were afraid I would go there to visit. I thought it somewhat weird while arousing my curiosity.

I secretly found your school through trial and error. I wanted to talk to your teacher about how you were getting along. I received very little information from you or your mother about school, or for that matter, even your health.

I introduced myself and said that I was there just to check on Angela Reisner and see how she was doing. They were confused because they had no one there by the name of Angela Reisner. The principal asked your teacher to come to the office and she said that your mother had told her, and thus the school, that Terry had adopted you or something like that and your name was Parn. I finally convinced them that Parn was not your name and later furnished proof. As far as I know, you used the name Angela Reisner from then on at that school. I think you only went to that private school for one year. I had seen the name Parn on other things like papers, emails and a soccer shirt. I knew what was going on. It bothered me greatly. The hyphenated name, *Reisner-Parn,* yet bothers me today.

Anyway, I got off the subject concerning why I was talking with Mr. Dearinger about you. He continued to ask questions about your summer visits. He asked me about how I disciplined you.

I asked, "what do you mean discipline. Are you talking about teaching, correcting or punishing?"

After all, I was a teacher for thirty years and know a little bit about disciplining. It's a lot more than punishing. Disciplining is *teaching self-discipline*, not punishing.

"I mean things like, do you talk to her, spank her, put her in a closet, things like that?" He asked.

I was shocked. I said, "Well, she is such a good kid and seldom does anything wrong. I guess when she does do something wrong it's glaring. All I have ever done is talk to her. We have talked about lying some, cheating on board games and being sort of a *know it all* and correcting me about things. We have discussed a few things. She has some definite ideas about religion, that is for sure, and we have disagreements. I have never done anything physical to her except hug her."

I continued, "Why are you asking me these questions?"

"Well, Angela has told a counselor in Georgia that you have abused her over the last several years during her summer visits."

He then went into detail about your allegations. I was shocked. I could not speak. I could not sit straight. It was as if someone had pounded me with a sledgehammer. He went on to describe what you told the counselor. I couldn't believe what he was reading from the Georgia report. I will not go into any of the details. They are accusations that I prefer to forget. They are accusations that I want you someday to be able to forget. I certainly don't want to broadcast them or put the report in one of these letters. Needless to say, the accusations were horrible.

I told him, "I could never do anything like that to anyone, much less my sweet daughter." I went on to say, "I have raised two other grown children and I never ever hurt them in anyway. I spanked my son really hard, when he was young and so was I, for catching one of my mother's dishtowels on fire with her cook stove."

I went on, "I believe that I did spank him too hard. I think that maybe I slapped my son and daughter once on a long camping trip to Washington, DC. It was when they were eight and ten years old. I regretfully remember doing it to this day. I so regretted it immediately."

I continued to reflect on that trip. "They don't remember it at all."

My daughter said when I mentioned it once, "We probably deserved it."

I continued, "I taught school for thirty years and there were never any complaints about me. I paddled one kid one swat in all those years. I have been married before and never hit, slapped or did anything like that to my wife. It's just crazy to think that I could do such a thing."

"It says here that you threw an ash tray into a wall once when arguing with Nancy," he read from the paper.

"I don't remember anything like that. I never really argued with Nancy because she always seemed to be the one with strong feelings. She was the one with the temper and I could not irritate her at all. She was explosive. She even made Jenny Hays, our eighty-year-old neighbor and good friend cry. Jenny had to tell Nancy to get her horses off Rock River Farm land, and if she needed help, the sherriff would come and help her. It had to do with her taking other people and other horses onto Jenny's land without permission. However, that is another story.

She once bragged that she pushed this six foot five two hundred and sixty pound man named Bill over a waterbed frame by poking him in the chest with her finger. He was the store manager where she worked as a salesperson. She, however, did have some advantage over him because her family owned the store he managed. She also told me that she once chased her brother Doug, trying to punch him, but Doug was too fast. I saw her temper many times. She used to say to people, "I'll be your worst nightmare," and they believed her.

"I did find it interesting in the report that she mentioned she would take a baseball bat to me. That seemed a little violent and like excessive force. She used to slap Angela because she wouldn't stand still when combing her hair. Her hair was difficult. I remember that. I used to have Angela watch TV in order to distract her when combing out hair knots. Angela's mother used to hit the dog with a wooden spoon. Oh, I could go on and on." I finally stopped talking, sitting motionless as he spoke. I didn't hear much of what he said. I was yet absorbing what he had said about the alleged abuse.

Maybe I shouldn't have told Mr. Dearinger all that stuff. Maybe I shouldn't tell you all this stuff. What I did say, however, indicated what a temper your mother has and of what kind of behavior she is capable. I saw that temper many times. I know you're no stranger to that temper.

I remember her telling me about growing up and how she would fight and how one time she smashed a windshield of a friend's boyfriend. Apparently he had mistreated her friend. I have seen her temper against other people, and then finally she turned it on me. I can't even go into how horrible she was when getting drunk. That is an altogether different story that I might go into later.

Ok, back to the meeting. I didn't know all of the allegations until I got the final report and saw them in print. I got it a few days later after the initial meeting. I went into shock again because of the details of which you spoke.

"Oh Angela," I kept saying because I felt so sorry for you and your troubled mind. I was so afraid for you. I thought that your mother was abusing you. I thought you were transferring it to me. I asked Mr. Dearinger at the meeting if he thought people ever transferred their abuse accusations onto other people. He told me he didn't have a degree in that sort of thing, that his degree was in Criminal Justice and he was just an investigator.

Wow, I thought, the same thing you are going to major in at college. How ironic is that?

"What do I do now?" I asked.

He couldn't give me any advice. I couldn't think straight. I finally decided that I could do nothing. I couldn't contact you because I didn't know what that might indicate. I couldn't reach out to you because I didn't know what could happen to me or how you would react. I figured the whole thing was in your court.

Mr. Dearinger told me that your mother was getting a restraining order so that I couldn't see, talk to or be around you. He told me that his report would go back to Georgia and that I would get a copy. He also said that if nothing happened in six months, he would shred the report. I finally left his office slowly and weakly. I was glad I didn't ride my motorcycle there that day. I'm not sure if I could have balanced it.

I have read the report several times and all the horrible details. I still cannot understand why you did it. I haven't received any kind of restraining paper and I haven't heard another word about the situation.

Debi said, "It's horrible and preposterous."

I finally told Brook and Kristen about the situation. They couldn't believe you could do such a thing, and later wrote letters saying what a great dad I was and how your allegations were cruel and wrong. Debi interviewed with Mr. Dearinger. He put her comments in his report.

You know if things went terribly wrong and if someone actually believed your allegations, I could have wound up in prison. I think you thought that your words would never leave that counselor's room. I cannot understand why your mother would say that she believes your allegations unless she is the abuser. I have worried and worried about you, Angela. I wish I could help you now. I write these letters not knowing what outcomes lay ahead. I have the report here in front of me. I will not include it in these letters. I don't want anyone else to read it.

Sincerely,

Dad

Beauty Has No Freedom

Forty white beads
fell from a
slender neck.
Forty loyal disciples
once silently slept.
An angelic obliging
host's treasure
scattered like rain in
liberating display.
Forty simple
sand grains
irritating nature,
created beauty.
Oysters wept and
died.
Pale white,
tinged with blue was
plucked.

Who slowly creates
durable beauty
in dark realms to be
brought forth distinctly
through innocent death?

Like shadows
over a sundial,
pearls slipped away.
Poised glory
could not escape
disappointment,
bound and
hung before
hungry eyes.
Pearls were

scattered
on a shiny
wooden floor.
Knotted string
followed,
finding freedom from
insecurity.

On aching knees,
someone gathered
beautiful symbols, and
in hand joined again
like brothers and
sisters those
far flung
lustrous spheres.
Strong tied string
again unified
social flaunting.
With passing time,
in drawer and
box, those
pearls silently
wait,
bound and
joined,
fastened and
secured.

Dear Angela – *Counselor*

I saw from the report that your mother was going to a counselor. He apparently wished to speak with you. It was a chance for you to speak your mind. You had no choice but to tell someone about your situation, real or not. I think you thought it would stay in that confidential room, but it couldn't. That is why Mr. Dearinger contacted me through the Tippecanoe County Child Services Department here in Lafayette.

I have been very afraid that your mother and Terry would have problems. I mean, he has given up most everything except his job for your mother, you and the other two kids. I mean your mother has everything she wants and needs. Yet, I also thought that about her when she lived in the big paid-for white house with free and clear horses and a husband with a good job and insurance. Oh well, the world changes and so do we, I guess. Anyway, I have been wishing that Terry would hang in there until you were at least out of college. I know that is selfish. Sorry. Actually except for taking you away, her leaving me was the best thing that could have happened. I met Debi and finally found true love. I sure hate it that you will not be around her anymore. She loves you like a daughter.

I saw in the report that your mother was originally going to the counselor. We looked him up on the Internet and found that he specializes in marriage counseling. We originally just wanted to know if he had a license and was qualified to work with people's minds, work with your mind.

You do know that Debi has a PhD in School Psychology and was a school psychologist for ten years in Lansing? I also have a Master's Degree in Education and taught for thirty years. I think that speaks a little bit about how we might be ones to ask questions about your upbringing and your schooling, but that never happened during all the separated years, especially given the fact that your mother barely got out of high school. I think we would have been a good source for child rearing advice.

I did see on the report that she claimed to be a college graduate and works in professional/technical areas. I also saw where she said I was unemployed when I'm actually retired. There's a big difference in being unemployed and being retired. There's also a big difference between barely making it out of high school and graduating from college. I hope that I don't seem to have a bad taste in my mental mouth.

Anyway, where was I? Oh, I was talking about the counselor. Debi wrote him a letter concerning our fear about abuse happening down there. I hope you are remaining safe. I do know that you're at an age where you could be combative against authority, against your mother. You're old enough to stand up for yourself, but I'm afraid if you push her too far, it could be not good for you. I hope you are being careful. If blaming me will keep you temporarily safe, then I don't mind, but eventually the truth will have to come out. Eventually you will have to shed yourself of the burden of lies. It must be a heavy load for you to carry, especially going to church so often and being such a strong Christian. I hope you reach out to the Holy Spirit. I know He will help you. Reach out!

Sincerely,

Dad

Dear Angela – *Debi*

I thought I might write a little bit, of what Mr. Dearinger included in his report after speaking to Debi. I don't know if you saw the report or not, but I doubt it.

Mr. Dearinger included that Debi has been in contact with you during the past five or more years. In fact, in September, we began our sixth year together. She told him that you were a well-behaved child who didn't need disciplining. She couldn't remember any time when I yelled at you. She said that there was never any need for physical discipline. She said that she had never seen any marks on you, as you alleged, and that she pretty much was around you 24/7; and when she went shopping or something like that, you usually went along.

You did like to hang around Debi a lot. You really love her, I know.

Debi stated that you might be making up these stories as a reason for not visiting. I disagreed, thinking there is something bad going on down there. I said that you already told a story to avoid coming to see us, that being the Jacksonville three week trip story. I, however, didn't think you went to Jacksonville for three weeks. Debi told Mr. Dearinger that I was a good father and told him about how I called and sent you cards almost every week.

I think Mr. Dearinger could ask a thousand people that know me if I'm capable of doing such things to anyone and they would say certainly, "no." I told Mr. Dearinger that he could question the five thousand or so students I had in school and he would get the same "no" answer about me being capable of abusing anyone. He would get a resounding "NO" everywhere he went.

It's unfair of you to do such a thing to anyone and especially your dad. It really can't hurt me anymore except if they throw me in jail.

I have my life record to stand on. There was a time when defending my reputation meant everything to me, but now it's not necessary or important. I don't have a job, boss or career to take care of. I don't need a standing in the community. My father told me that my name and reputation were very important and to take care of them. I took care of them. I yet take care of them even though I don't need to.

"Your reputation is based on your actions," he used to say.

I never forgot what he told me. I thought I had taught you that also. I know Brook and Kristen learned many lessons from me. I pray those lessons are also deep down inside of you.

When I was giving Brook all those "how to behave" lectures, I wasn't sure he was listening, but years later, he is following my advice. He was listening after all just as I was listening to my dad. I wonder if my dad questioned whether I was listening or not. Brook has gone on to put into practice those lessons that I learned and passed on. I wonder if those lessons came from my great grandfather. Maybe those lessons even came from the old country, Germany. Wow, that's a thought.

Sincerely,

Dad

Dear Angela – *Afraid for You*

This whole thing about abuse has gotten us to wondering why you have had several accidents down there, concerning mostly your horses, and have not gone to the doctor. You have gone to a doctor for other problems. Why have you not gone to the doctor for some serious injuries?

I remember when you had most assuredly a concussion and were not taken to the doctor. You told me that you had bad headaches for nearly a week. I said, "You should go to the doctor, especially when you have good insurance."

I don't know of any parent who doesn't take their kid to the doctor when seriously hurt, and especially when having good insurance. Didn't you also break an arm and had a broken ankle?

I remember you telling me about two of your horses kicking you in the chest. I would think that was a great reason to go to the hospital for an x-ray. It seems like you would have been hurt from that incident. You could have had broken ribs or even something more serious. I don't remember or probably don't even know all your injuries.

It scares me to think that your mother never took you to the doctor any of those times. I ask, "Why?"

It scares me now that you might not go when you really should go to the doctor. Most parents will not take a chance on their child being badly hurt. In fact, they usually take their children to get a checkup or an x-ray too often. I would surely think your mother would take you to the doctor especially due to your health conditions.

I certainly would have taken you when up here if you got hurt. Remember that time you had a sore throat and I immediately took you to the doctor. I would have done the same for any illness or injury. I think it is strange about the no doctor thing. I hope those injuries were not results of abuse. I worry about you. Debi worries about you also. She is a great female model for you to study. She has a lot of knowledge to share with you; after all, she did raise three girls. I think that alone makes her an expert on girl stuff.

Sincerely,

Dad

195

My Heart Speaks

Does a prayer
speak my mind or
does my heart best
speak for
itself a prayer?
I pray thankfully,
sorrowfully, fearfully
because I can.
I have much, but
what about those
who have little?
How much better
they pray than me.
Seems less is
more again as I
study those with
little and a lot.
Seems a prayer
given by one
who has nothing is
authentic and
sincere.
Seems much of
everything gets in
reluctant way of
realizing only little
something is needed.
Does a prayer
speak my mind?
I nearly don't notice
I am praying.
A true prayer is
given without
conscious thought.
Best prayers are

given with few
spontaneous words.

Does my heart
best speak for
itself a prayer?
I don't have to
always moan fear and
destruction.
I only need a
heart speaking for
itself.
Does structure of
prayer mean
anything?
Are not my prayers
translated to
He who is
above
my ignorance?

Dear Angela – *Hope*

I have not heard from you for several months. Here it is the middle of October. I was thinking about Christmas the other day and how you probably won't be here. I think about you every day. I talked to Brook once and Kristen several times about you and your situation. You know, you are also cutting them out of your life by cutting me out. They love you for sure. Debi and I often talk about you and many of the things we did together.

Debi was and yet is a great friend to you, Angela. I know you reached out to her and needed her female companionship when together. I can't help but think you also need a different kind of woman in your life besides your mother. She gives you only one model of a woman, wife and mother to study. I think you need Debi and me a lot more than we need you. We are pretty much, what we are, but you are still becoming what you will become. People love as others love them. We love you very much. You are changing and learning so much these days. We want to be a part of your learning process. It is another critical time in your life.

I'm in limbo with no answers coming and no hope for the future concerning pulling us back together. I sent you my first book before this happened. I hope you read it and learned a little more about what is going on inside my head. You already know what kind of person I am.

I'm going to get my own website after I publish my third book. I already have my domain name, AN AMERICAN POET, *anamericanpoetcom.com.*

Sincerely,

Dad

Sway and Confirmation

Judgment sway
seeks confirmation,
wind seeks direction and
storms need a
bad behaving
place to vent.

How can a man
not be likewise in
his survival quest?
In sought days and
life lost moments,
his judgment sways
seeking solidity.

How much freedom
can a man relinquish
without a fight?
How many days
can pass without
sunlight before a
garden wilts and dies?

Middle ground is
hard to reach.
A place is
needed where
all is satisfied;
where all is
confirmed, and
becomes soft,
pliable and
discovered.

Judgment always has
direction.
Consensus decides
where to place
flowers and
vegetables alike.

Notice how
they grow
towards life giving
sun.
Notice how
confirmation
makes life's struggle
continue.

Colorful Wings

We silently sit
face to face,
looking into eyes with
open hearts and minds.
You are Tuesday light and
Wednesday polished brass.
I am grainy oak wood and
blue lining velvet.
Our relationship is
butterfly wings and
white cirrus clouds.
We come together
knowing ourselves
in an understanding place.
Wonder greets as
faith soothes while
peace prevails.
We are trumpet and
wooden case,
exploring beautiful music.
We are colorful wings,
flying effortlessly high.

CHAPTER VII

Spirit Connecting

Dear Angela – *Other Children*

I thought I would write some about how much my other children love me. I'm not bragging or talking about something that I only think is true. I know they love me. I also know that you love me.

I don't hold any grudge against you. I yet love you just as much as always. Do you remember our last conversation when I was telling you about my feelings towards you? That was before I found out about what you did.

I said, "I'll always be your father. I'll be the only real father you'll ever have and you will be my daughter forever."

That has not changed and will not change. It is unconditional love that I have for you, sometimes also referred to as *Grace*.

I just hope nothing happens to us before you have a chance to apologize and set the story truthfully straight. I don't think it will mean anything to me when I'm gone, but I fear it will mean much to you after I'm gone. Think about that.

I'm going to include the letters from Brook and Kristen. I will scan and insert them exactly as written.

Sincerely,

Dad

Brook's letter:

Sir/Madam

Recently I was made aware of solemn accusations concerning my father, Phillip Reisner. Purpose of this note is an attempt to convey, in a small amount of sentences, my relationship with my father.

At the age of nine, my parents separated. My sister and I remained with our Mother. At eleven I asked, and was granted, the opportunity to live with my Father. We resided together until eighteen. During that time, he began to instill within me what hard work and determination meant—honesty and the willingness to study and learn. Throughout those years, he was there for everything that I needed. My father was always patient with me, spent any amount of time working with me on whatever I needed and never abused me. Ever.

I can say without equivocation that I knew he loved me. Then and now.

One of the many traits he possesses is patience, a trait that I still struggle with today. I was diagnosed with Hyperactivity back then, many would call AD/HD today. Our first challenge when I moved in was the elimination of the medication I was taking. Not once during those taxing years did my father strike me or mistreat me. Again showing patience and resolve parenting me.

In 1999 I asked my father to be my best man at my wedding. That was the first and only way I would be able to show him how much he has meant to me. I am the man that I am today because of him.

Finally, the allegations levied toward my father stem from nefarious individuals with whom Angela surrounds herself. Certainly they are unfounded and do not represent who my Father truly is.

Regards,

Brook Reisner

Stones On My Path

A small card left at my door,
opened a world of feared hurt.
I stepped through a
doorway and later
into an unfamiliar room.
I left comfort zone and
stepped into a world of fear,
hurt and sympathy.
In a few moments
I discovered something of
which I had no control.
My innocence could not
pave a road towards
understanding.
I was left sitting in
amazement with no
vehicle to drive towards
accusation correcting.
False maps and
misdirected words
scattered mind confusion.
I could not stand or
lean well and wished to
grasp an absent hand.
I could not hear or
see well as words and
instructions directed towards me
passed without collection.
I then walked a new path,
strewn with adversity,
rough as a new
created path that
I wished not to walk.
That small printed card,

*fostered hurtful words and
false accusations,
drove me to tears.
How can a sweet
innocent mind get damaged
so well as to make a path
requiring redemption?
Stones laid on my path,
struck me first on their way
towards earth.
I shall never walk same
path with sore feet and
wobbly mind.
My future is
unknown.*

Kristen's letter:

To Whom This May Concern,

I am the daughter of Phillip Dale Reisner. He is my biological father and sole father figure for my entire life. We lived in the same household for almost eight years prior to divorce from my mother, Babs Reisner. After the divorce I consistently stayed with him on Sundays, Wednesday evenings and vacation time throughout the year.

I would like to state on record what type of father my dad was and is today. He is a man of great character and trustworthiness. He is kind, patient and loving.

He cares deeply for his children and would do anything for them. He taught us how to work hard, demonstrate integrity and relish time off from work and school.

He has never been violent towards me as a child or as an adult. He has always conducted himself with self control and calmness. Any claims made against him to the contrary are shocking, upsetting and hard to believe. If I felt there was any threat of violent behavior either verbally or physically I would never allow my three children to be around him. He has my full trust, support and love. My father and I have remained close throughout childhood and adulthood. He is a huge blessing to me and my family. We are grateful for his love. If you have any questions please contact me at 303.805.5258.

Sincerely,

Kristen Carlson

Dear Angela – *Debi's Letter*

Dear Dr. Montes:

I am writing in response to the recent Investigation of Alleged Child Abuse against Phillip Reisner by his daughter, Angela Reisner. It is my understanding that Angela had/has been seeing you for therapy and that, in conversations with you, the allegations of abuse first surfaced. I have had the opportunity to review the report by Justin Dearinger from the Indiana Department of Child Services and admit that I was incredulous of Angela's testimony against her father. I have been a part of Angela's life for the past five years and have witnessed first-hand the compassionate and caring relationship between Angela and her father. Never in my experience have I seen Phil raise a hand against Angela, and I have been present almost constantly when Angela comes to visit. In fact I have never witnessed any act of physical or verbal aggression by Phil, and everyone who knows Phil (including his grown daughter, Kristen) finds the allegations to be unbelievable. Each year we keep a photo-journal of Angela's experiences, documenting the places that we have visited and the things we have done as a family. Phil has carefully and lovingly recorded trips and everyday events with little notes and messages of remembrance.

As we have gone back over these albums, we are struck by how happy Angela seems in the photos.

I spoke with my daughter who works for the National Domestic Violence Hotline in Austin, Texas because I needed to know why a child would fabricate these charges. One possibility that she suggested was that Angela was actually experiencing abuse in her mother's home while choosing to displace her fears onto her father because of the safety in distance. The other possibility that she entertained was that Angela simply did not want to visit her dad this summer because of her other commitments with horse camps and events. She may have made up the allegations because she did not want to tell Phil directly that she wanted to stay at home for her activities. I do not have any evidence of abuse by her mother or step-father from my interactions with Angela so I would hope to believe the second explanation.

Regardless, it would seem that these alternate explanations might be explored in therapy.

As you can imagine, these allegations have been devastating to both Phil and myself. We love Angela deeply and are saddened that she would resort to false claims against us. Our hearts go out to her for whatever she is suffering, and we only want to know why she appears to be hurting so deeply. While Mr. Dearinger concluded that the allegations were unsubstantiated in his report, I still wanted to

contact you with this letter so that you are aware of my interpretation of the situation. Anyone who knows Phil who has learned of this investigation is in total disbelief. I know that you are unable to confirm that you are seeing Angela, and I respect the privacy of the therapeutic relationship. I

simply offer this letter as a gesture of concern from a dad and a step-mom who love Angela very much.

Sincerely,

Deborah Bennett

Dear Angela – *Dealing With Hardship*

I can't relay to you how much we love you. I know you have always had a little problem about truth and playing fair, but you are yet a wonderful person. I admire you for being able to cope with life, be strong and positive no matter what the situation. You have been through so much besides losing your identical twin sister.

It is finally possible for me to write about our horrible loss of Kaitlyn. I've never had to endure anything that bad before or since. It's the worst thing to happen to a parent. I can't imagine what it has been like for you. I think because you were so young, it was hard to understand well, but then again, I think you got help from Jesus and the Holy Spirit. Maybe it wasn't as bad for you as it could have been. I can't make any kind of judgment for you. We never really talked about it. I think we both just didn't want to bring it up.

We learned that Kaitlyn didn't have a spleen and then found out that you also don't have a spleen. I remember when we went to Methodist Hospital and you had that nuclear imagining. I guess the spleen is very difficult to find because it lies on or near the liver. We found out that you have only a remnant of a spleen. I prayed for three years that Jesus would give you my spleen or for yours to grow again. I knew it would be a miracle for us, but only a simple thing for Him to perform. I guess He wasn't of a mind to say "yes."

We finally found through blood tests that nothing had changed concerning your spleen, so I gave up on that prayer. You later got a vaccination and I prayed a new prayer. I asked that you be safer and more protected because of the vaccination.

We never let down on diligence concerning bacteria. We washed our hands constantly, watched for sick people and didn't go to public places much. I screened playmates to make sure they were not the least bit sick. I also monitored myself for germs and bacteria. There was no end to our vigilance. You couldn't fight bacteria without a spleen very well and the penicillin you took daily didn't help that much. That was a fact. We knew this and had to live accordingly. I yet worry about bacteria. I still wash my hands all the time even when you're not around. It's nice that you can now do a lot more than you could in those early days.

You have also had to deal with those condromas and I know they have been painful. I feel for your condition all the time. Then the arthritis came up to confound your health further. The original doctor at Methodist thought that you wouldn't have arthritis until you were older, around fifty or sixty I think he said. Well, he was wrong for sure and now here you are coping with that. You have been so brave with all the negative things that have happened to you. No wonder you are a bit confused. I think Debi helped us to be a real family while you were here. Remember our toast at dinnertime, "Here's to us?" That was great, and we prayed at the dinner table when you were here. You were a good influence on us. I pray we can share influences again.

We are like separate words put into a sentence, then placed in a stone wall crack for a little while. We are like a love letter sent by God, accumulating and fulfilling life. We are our memories and experiences serving as mortar that hold our lives together. We are like building stones held together until passing time erodes our spirits and carries us back to heaven.

Sincerely,

Dad

Hoeing Weeds

When minds conjure
destructive evil thoughts
like acid rain contaminating
fertile soil,
actions harm as if
stealing goods and
destroying beliefs.
Enraged
shouting beings
blame and excuse
not selves, while
weedy thoughts
kill and maim
nestled garden flowers.
To understand
thinking is to
understand
gardening.
To understand
weeding is to
understand
preservation.
Another mind
singing,
another cloud
breaking,
another soul
bleeding
must be found.
Earth grows
weeds.
Evil exists in
flowering minds.
Rain blesses
sunshiny days.

Weeds insist
own destructive
ways.
Hoeing ways,
mind conjure
strength,
thoughts are
controlled,
soil is
preserved,
humanity whispers
His name.

Dear Angela – *Collecting Nuts*

Today the sun is out and it is cool. I look out the window at the big hickory tree, remembering all those nuts you and Debi collected that one summer. There has never been a year quite like that one, with so many nuts. I wish I could remember if there were more nuts or if the squirrels didn't bother with them that year because it was going to be a mild winter.

Well, the past two years for sure have been rather nut-less. The squirrels have gathered all of them. Last year was cold for quite some time. Maybe they know the future weather picture after all. They collected all the nuts again this year. What does that mean?

I think Mother Nature is a little bit scatterbrained. She has a hard time making up her mind about the weather, but she is very consistent about flowers and trees, mountains and seas, men and beasts. It's just a matter of how she treats everything with wind, water and temperature. I guess it's rather simple when you think about it, and to think it all comes down to her sun.

When it comes to humans, I think it all comes down to love. It's how we treat everyone with our own wind, water and temperature provided by "The Son."

Sincerely,

Dad

Deaf and Faithful

Oh, Lord make me
more than I am.
Make me realize
I am less than thought.
Let me know what
you wish me to be.
Let me do
what you will.
Let me feel
what you speak.
Let wisdom and
truth
cross my path.
Let me hear those
three words aloud,
"I accept you."
And if not possible,
let my heart be
strong enough to
remain deaf and
faithful.

Dear Angela – *Beautiful Clowns*

Of course, life goes on as I make plans for tomorrow, next month and next year. I sit here recalling how you have grown. I got some pictures out from the bookshelf, looking for that particular one at Riley Hospital with the clown standing behind us. I can't find it. Maybe it's like some of those memories of yours. It was something I only needed at the time. Maybe it was one of those "signs," that I didn't heed. I can't help but think about that picture occasionally.

I remember your mother said that Kaitlyn kept saying,

"Look at all the beautiful clowns," when she was going to the doctor and then at the hospital.

I think she was delirious from her temperature, but I also think that there was something going on concerning the spiritual world. I have often thought that those clowns were actually angels. I mean, how would Kaitlyn have known what an angel looks like, for that matter, how would any one of us know what an angel looks like? I believe in my heart that those clowns were indeed angels and they were comforting, leading and teaching her about the future. I think she was in transition when she left our house heading for the doctor, heading for the hospital, heading for heaven.

I believe that I have sometimes felt angels near me, but have never seen one. Maybe I have seen a picture of one. Maybe that clown standing behind us at Riley was an angel. I bet there are many angels flying around the rooms and halls of Riley Hospital. I bet that place is angel crowded. They are probably bumping into each other. I surely felt them in that neonatal intensive care unit at Methodist Hospital. I can nearly feel them now.

Kaitlyn was certainly sick that night and the next morning. They said she died from Streptopneumococis A, or blood poisoning. She couldn't fight the bacteria without a spleen.

I often wonder why you didn't get sick also. You had the same exposure that day. I think that you were not as near to that sick boy as Kaitlyn. You didn't befriend him, take his hand and make him feel wanted. Then again, maybe someone was protecting you. Maybe Kaitlyn was destined to pass from Earth early and you are not.

You must continue to live for yourself and for Kaitlyn. You must remain strong and endure what comes your way. You must be honest, live boldly and have faith that everything will be all right. I'm sure you know better than me that you need to lean on the Holy Spirit. He is the One that will never let us down.

Sincerely,

Dad

Dear Angela – *Collecting Memories*

I am sure you remember the scrapbooks we put together and I used to keep for you. You helped some, but I mostly kept them going. We used to collect little bits and pieces of evidence of our adventures. We collected some crazy things, and they are all in the scrapbooks. I looked at them some the other day. I'm amazed at what all is in them. The pictures are great. Most of them are before Debi gave me the digital camera for my birthday. We finally got a good printer, so now we can print more pictures. I do have many pictures on CD's that are in scrapbooks. The thing now is that we're not keeping scrapbooks anymore. We're collecting little and thus have little to put in them. I still keep scrapbooks for Debi and myself. Your stuff is with our stuff now.

I'm sure you'll want them some day. Maybe they don't interest you much right now, but I bet they will later be like precious jewels. They're sort of that way for me now. You have looked at them some when here during the summer. I guess they aren't completely boring to you. I would like to give them to you some day.

Sincerely,

Dad

Oval Mirror

You gaze into an
oval mirror to
see yourself as
others might, but
reflected image,
through own eyes,
reveals a distorted figure.
Your eager eyes are
like seeing through
second hand glasses.

Youth blinds with
heat, then cools with
dusky age.
Your image is
always changing.
It wavers as if
washed and cleaned,
pinned on a
clothes line, but
will not dry.

Your image is
like a wingless bird,
waterless fountain,
motherless child.
A mirror betrays and
never speaks.
Truth is in your
mind's eye and
perception in your
askew soul.

Perhaps you should
seldom look into a
mirror and
see yourself only
softening with time.
For in distorted
image, a
dragon lies and
eats ego fantasy for
lunch.

Spiritual world
lies at
mirror's surface,
within depth
beyond material
glass and silver.
Be content with
infrequent earthly
oval mirror
gazes.

I'm Just a Rose Waiting

You're a red rose in
evening dim light
appearing black in a
silent empty room.
You're inadequate and
love speak lost.
You might as well be a
stem placed
dried petal bundle.
But, you think all
needed is a
revealing
switched on
radiant light.

Illuminating light
cannot revive life, nor
darkness destroy love.
Worthiness cannot
consume usefulness.
Rose memories are like
love notes read and
forgotten in
gray approaching night.
You yet remember how
beautiful you are
in morning's light with
dew droplet petals and
water surging stems.

Dear Angela – *But She Loves You*

I saw Jan Cook the other day and she asked about you. I didn't know quite what to say, so I finally told her what was happening between us. She was shocked, Angela. She couldn't understand why you would accuse me of child abuse. She has known me for forty years and, you, all your life.

She said, "But she loves you so much. I've seen that love."

"I think so too. She told me that she loved me the last time I talked to her on the phone, but I'm not sure if she told those lies before or after she called."

Venita also asked me about you and I told her about your actions. She was flabbergasted. I just don't know what to tell people when they ask about you.

I have not gone by Helen Shilling's house lately because I don't want to lie to her. She always wants to know how and what you are doing. Do I say that you are ok or having health problems or what? I just won't know what to say when I see her.

I don't lie, but I don't really want to tell the truth. I just wish you could clear this whole thing up and we could go back to being loving, friendly and truthful. I really want things the way they were. I can't condone your behavior, and I can't reach out to you. I don't know where my inaction will take me.

Our future is in your hands.

Sincerely,

Dad

Dear Angela – *Christmas*

The next holiday coming after your destructive allegations is Christmas. That is a time when I would normally see you. I remember so many wonderful Christmases when you were happy to come to Indiana, and always hoping for snow. You were always hoping for sledding with Debi on the big Purdue hills, the big icy Purdue hills. Especially that particular icy one that scared you at first, but once you got used to it, you became a daredevil. Oh, then there was the trying to slide on our driveway with the cookie sheet. You were desperate for equipment. That was before we finally got a cheap sled. You bent it all up trying to slide down the driveway. It, however, still bakes good cookies.

There were those times when I put up the tree and you decorated it. We did that even before Debi was with us. You always liked to decorate the tree. I always had plenty of decorations. I sure will miss you this Christmas.

Debi and I are going to Florida for a couple of months after Christmas. I wish you were going with us for a few days again this year. That was a fun five days last year. Ok, we found it a little bit tight in the travel trailer, but it was great being together. We will have a condo this year with plenty of room.

Sincerely,

Dad

CHAPTER VIII

Road Realizing

Dear Angela – *Movie*

I watched a movie last night. It provoked thinking much about Kaitlyn and you. It was about a fifteen-year-old girl who lost her life at the hands of a freak, a mentally ill killer. I know Kaitlyn didn't go through anything like that, but she was about your and Kaitlyn's age. The girl in the movie reminded me of you. I guess that was what moved me to think about you. She had a personality kind of like yours.

I have thanked God many times that Kaitlyn went peacefully and without violence. I see that violent stuff on TV and could just cry. The movie also provoked thinking about you not being with me. I know we didn't get to see each other a lot, but we were yet together in spirit. We were in contact. We were pals, I thought, as well as father and daughter.

I don't know how long you have known that you were not my biological daughter, but I suspect a lot longer than I realize. I don't know why or how you learned about it, but to me it doesn't matter. It didn't matter to the Indiana University Medical Center, the courts or me. IU said you were my daughter for life. No questions asked. Anyway, I will always be your father and you my daughter. No one can take that away from us.

Oh, yes, about the movie. It was a very spiritual movie. I didn't like the ending because no one got revenge. However, it was like God says, "Revenge is mine," and that was how it ended. The killer fell off a snowy cliff while trying to get another girl into his car. He had killed several girls all about the same age and they were all in the movie. They were spirits waiting to go to heaven. I guess they were sort of like in transition. The girl, of whom I'm speaking, took them to heaven with her after God took His revenge. They were all set free from the waiting place.

It was sad thinking about how young, innocent and vulnerable you are, and thinking about how Kaitlyn never got a real chance in life. She, however, did have a lot of influence while here. I think she made a mark on the world. I think she also escorted you into the world, leading the way, and finally giving you some of her traits. I think by being mirror twins, in the final analysis, you now have shared traits with her.

That movie was different from you girls. The girl in the movie was only 15 years old, but she still reminded me a little of you. You know: good looking, smart and hardworking. It provoked those protective emotions that I possess concerning you. Kaitlyn is in heaven and you are here. I must concentrate on you. Forgive me if I am selfish.

Sincerely,

Dad

Life Crumbles

I'm faltering words
In a wall,
Dusty paper scrolled.
Scarred road maps
Show meaning on
Bloody callused hands.
Fear causes
Storm sounds in
Head, Mind and
Gray heart.

Crumbling words,
Like heavy tears,
Speak and
Send me farther and
Deeper than ever.
I am a stone
Within a wall of
Head, Mind and
Gray heart.

Living erodes,
Grinds and destroys.
I crumble cry,
Strength isn't and
Structure won't.
I'm architect piled,
Stone stacked with
Critical mortar of
Head, Mind and
Gray heart.

Dear Angela – *Protecting Self*

I have never been able to write about Kaitlyn's death until now. I have tried several times. Now with the temporary loss of you, I have gained renewed courage and understanding. I see how Jesus took Kaitlyn away with God's permission, but now I see the Devil trying to take you away, but surely without God's permission. The Devil will not win. I know your estrangement from me is temporary. I know that you will someday make things right and that you will, even if rarely, be back with Debi and me again.

We had our train trip planned for Colorado and everyone out there was excited to see us all. I can't help but think that you are having too little control over what is happening. I think you are protecting yourself. I am waiting for you to make some kind of move and we will finally take that Colorado trip one way or another.

God bless you.

Sincerely,

Dad

Witness

Liberty eternally strives
in souls given by a higher being,
thoughtfully construed through
timeless creative arrangement.
Each being represents humanity and
shall not be specified less soul
than another; for significant souls
bear witness to God's wisdom and
life's fashion.

Earth seeks day, season and
year autonomy as plants expand
necessary foliage whether
wispy ounce or weighty pound.
Its root burrows downward while
flora reaches upward.
No weed or flower is given
less soul than another through
God's wisdom and life's fashion.

A long forgotten cistern and
hand pump have no definition or
remembrance for young or old.
Time is a knowledge circle
repeating soul and
remembering seed.
Thirst never loses
its defining moment through
God's wisdom and life's fashion.

Dear Angela – *Wondering*

Debi and I think about you often and wonder what you're doing at a particular time. We talk about your health, whether you are in school or not and whether you are able to ride your horses. We discussed just this morning, whether you are listening to the Holy Spirit and if your conscience is working.

I ask, "If you are listening and He is speaking, are you having a rough time coping?"

We frequently wonder what is going on in your life and in the life of your mother and Terry. We looked up your counselor on the internet and found that he is mainly a divorce counselor. We suspect that he asked you to talk with him because of problems at home. I think he must have asked you some very pointed questions, questions that had to do with your home life. He must have asked you questions about being happy.

I have a feeling that you figured that anything said would be confidential and nothing would leave that room. Well, little did you know that false accusations about me abusing you would not stay in that room. Those accusations could have put me in deep trouble. Your claims are very serious. I hope you know by now that being a false witness is a crime. It could have changed my whole world. The counselor had no choice but to report your accusations to the Child Services Department. Ok, now seemingly everything was out. The only thing is that everything was a lie concerning me. You must have either sighed in relief or gasped in fear. You had put yourself in a bad spot.

"What will happen now?" you must have asked yourself or did you have any idea what the consequences might be. I suspect the latter.

I have thought all along that you're transferring the abuse onto me rather than the real person. I hesitate to point a finger, but I think the abuser is your mother. I also believe that someone was abusing your mother as a child.

She told me a story about laying unconscious on the bathroom floor after a hitting incident and no one called for help or took her to the doctor. Does that sound familiar? I think there are other telling stories.

I have seen her temper and her reaction towards others who have gone against her will. I can name several people who have felt her intimidation: big strong men, customers, little old women and supposedly good friends.

She, however, used that intimidation skill to get information from the doctor who performed Kaitlyn's autopsy. She had to intimidate the funeral home director, Tom Hunt, to get the name and phone number of the doctor. That probably saved your life because he was the one who discovered that Kaitlyn had no spleen and gave your mother that information. He advised us to find out promptly if you had a spleen after learning that Kaitlyn had a twin sister. We then learned how to protect you from bacteria. I wish we had known that you both had no spleen earlier. So, I guess your mother's mean, tough personality paid off at least one time.

Anyway, I fear for your well-being. I fear that if these things are true in your home, they are bad and could escalate into something worse. I can't think of something worse than a knife to the throat, as you described in your accusations, except a knife cutting the throat.

Sincerely,

Dad

Dear Angela – *Spring Journey*

I wrote this book, *Mountain Peak Jumper*, a long time ago. I think I mentioned it in a previous letter. I wrote it as a novel, but it wasn't very good. I've since converted it into a book of poems. I now think it is pretty good. Of course, that is up to the critics. The book is about ready for print. I've edited, rewritten and tweaked it for quite some time now. I think that maybe it will be the next book I publish.

It's about a golden eagle who takes a journey far from home. You see, golden eagles usually only travel approximately six miles from their home nest and they are generally not brave at all, as compared to the American bald eagle who is fierce. This particular golden eagle somehow has human memories and attributes. This unusual phenomenon has to do with the spiritual world and the idea that human beings possess a transitional spirit, mind and soul that is rooted in God's essence. These three hidden intangibles, spirit, mind and soul, are unlike body, brain and chemical composition. We cannot find or touch spirit, mind and soul; but they are vastly more important than touchable body, brain and chemical composition. The eagle's name is Rouker and he travels throughout the southwestern corner of Utah. I have drawn a map of his sojourn. I could show it to you some time.

Well, Debi and I are planning to take that same journey early this coming summer. The thing is, we have to get out there before we can take the trip. We have to take a trip in order to take a trip. We're going to take the long way getting there. We're going to tent camp much of the time and also visit family via Memphis, Tennessee to see Brook, Austin, Texas to see Alisha, St George, Utah to see Rouker, Denver, Colorado to see Kristen and then back to Lafayette, Indiana to see Kiddy-Kidee.

It's about a forty-five hundred mile journey. I will take enough pictures to visually record the journey and then include enough poems to describe my observations. I would then like to put the pictures with poems in a book. The books that I've presently written are poems that include black and white pictures. This book would include color pictures with corresponding poems. I think it will be quite an adventure and hopefully a future book. Of course, this is only possible because Debi is going on phased or half-year retirement.

She is teaching this semester, but will not during the summer and fall semester.

It would be nice if you could go with us. I know you like to tent camp, and staying with family along the way will make it a little easier. I'm excited about it. We figure it will take about three weeks and we can't wait. It's as I said in an earlier letter; heaven and earth won't wait on sand grains to shift. The desert is covertly shifting without our awareness. Debi and I are the sand grains in this case. We are doing it because we can and before it is too late.

Sand grains are unimportant in an important desert, but without each and every one, the desert would certainly be less. We are seemingly unimportant, but to the humanitarian desert, we are very important. I think most people feel unimportant. They are aware of self-importance only through selfish and self-preservation reasons, but fail to understand that they are most important in the grand spiritual scheme of things. All the unimportant parts make up the important whole. God would be less without each one of us.

It is, however, others in our lives that make us truly important and that is by remembering relationships. We become important as others elevate our importance. That is partly why I am writing these letters, remembering our wonderful experiences together and letting you know how important you are to me. I also don't want you to forget me.

I'm humbly reporting some partial history in these letters, not because I did anything special, caused grand memories or taught anyone how to be a wonderful human being, but just for own posterity of life. I'm hoping you will learn a few more lessons through these letters that I should have taught you. All I wanted was to help transplant a few little spiritual specks of God in this world.

Sincerely,

Dad

Be a Rock

Perspective is a time
management teacher.
If a person doesn't have it,
much is a surprise.
Too many surprises
change perspective.
A stone is a stone until
pressed into concrete service, and
then it becomes a
hidden entity seeking freedom.
Stones never cry and
concrete slabs never say sorry.
In perspective, both
need a place to belong;
both need someone to
put them in a useful place.
Seek and you will find
keeps a young man happy with
faith and hope.
Faith can drive a person crazy
unless not having some.
Hope can drive a person angry
with too much.
Stone tyrants on
mountain peaks
have no mercy.
They slide faith and hope
down mountain sides until
there is concrete courage
no more.

Dear Angela – *Thinking About You*

I doubt that you watch the news much. It never seemed to interest you much. I'm a news crazy type of guy as you know and I've been watching the Obama administration trying to ruin the country. It seems everything he does harms the country.

Anyway, I think this coming election is going to be a turning point in our country. I hope we can start to take back our rights and responsibilities planned for us in the Constitution. We must return to the original beliefs of the Founding Fathers. I think your future depends on it. I doubt that what is happening now will affect me much, but your future happiness is in jeopardy. I think you should look into today's politics. It's hard to believe that you are only a few months from voting age. In fact, you missed being eligible to vote by only a few months last time.

I was also thinking about you driving, wondering if you're driving to school. I know you thought you would this fall. I don't even know if you are attending college. I looked at your Facebook postings and saw where you said you were going to Dalton State, but of course, I don't know that for sure. I would like to know what is going on in your life. I wish I could send you this letter, and then get an answer.

Ok, until then I will leave it here in this future book. Maybe someday I'll hand the letters or the *Letters to Angela* book to you. The letters show my weaknesses, flaws and ignorance. I seek to improve myself, but I'm afraid the cup is old, and full of cracks and chips.

Sincerely,

Dad

Potter's Cup

My potter's cup,
once earthen mud,
shaped with
artful grace,
adorned and
kiln fired
got dropped.

It, like myself
begs more life,
more days filled with
sweet drink.
It begs for
something to
drift mind and
muddle brain to
think abstract
thoughts
in moon lit
night air.
It wishes
something to
cause leaping
over hell's
threatening gates.
It needs
something to
make an
intrepid soul
fly like a goose on
water's edge.

My potter's cup,
once useful,
now lies in inept

scattered blur on a
cold surface.
My nearly silent
soul lies painfully
waiting
emergency service.
I need someone to
help broken me
find new life
as might a
fix-it man repair
my potter's cup.

Repair me for
I am at a
desperate point and
speak forgiving words.
Echoing halls
require white angel
coats and blue
spirit surgeon garb.

Mend me as if a
potter's cup, so that
I might with
calloused hands and
weathered mind,
surely create another
artful new goblet.
Help my brothers
commune with a
new cup or even a
repaired cup, and
celebrate a
fresh beginning with
wine and bread.

Dear Angela – *Introspection*

With all this writing of letters and poetry to you, I have been thinking much. It's good to get some thinking off my mind and onto paper.

I have considered our relationship, my relationship with Debi and my relationship with my family. These letters have become a book for sure. I wish I had more space, but I don't want it to be huge. This book is for you and if others wish to read it, they will honor me. I hope you will enjoy and learn from it.

I have also thought about myself, how I learned to be a free honest person who wishes to simplify life. I thought about how my father could say much with a few simple words. A good example would be when I was sixteen and going out in my car.

He would say, "Be careful and behave."

That meant a whole paragraph and I had to do some serious thinking concerning what he meant by "behave." It was also the way in which he said behave that drew my attention. We had discussed the subject of behaving many times while sitting on the front porch or walking the fields of corn and soybeans. I knew what he meant. I just had to think about applying it.

Another short sentence would be, "Make me proud and don't disappointment me."

Now that put a lot of pressure on me to be a good person. We discussed pride and approval many times on that same screened porch.

My mother also talked and taught by example many lessons. A good illustration is how when Henry Boyle, the father of a good friend of my dad, lost his wife at seventy-five years old and he wished not to live any longer himself. He wouldn't eat. My mother baked and took two pies to him every week for several months. He basically only ate her apple and cherry pies. He gradually started eating other foods that she took to him. He eventually assumed care of himself and lived another ten years because of my mother's care and loving attention. She did many things like that.

These are example of how my parents raised me. Parents, friends and teachers influence our upbringing. Please let me help you.

All that we have experienced, learned and felt is stored in our soul, mind and spirit. We must look inside ourselves for answers, for wisdom. Introspection is a self-examination process that gathers feelings and thoughts waiting for our scrutiny. It takes time and effort. It is sometimes painful and awkward. It is sometimes joyous and effortless.

Sincerely,

Dad

I Smile

I rise today
before daybreak.
Dim eastern light
whispers of
impending morning.
Mystery fills
my eyes as
slight breeze
caresses trees.
My world pretends to
sleep as if
waiting on me.
And yet
I know in
heart it is ever
changing, growing,
dying like small,
innocent, insignificant me.
We are seemingly same
except I am here a
second and
Earth a lifetime.
Brevity is my truth,
longevity my prayer.
In one second
I confirm existence and
purpose to God.
In one second
I hear Earth speak
good morning and
I smile.

CHAPTER IX

Letters Ending

Dear Angela – *Some Personal History*

I'm taking some space to write about myself a little bit and share some personal history that you don't know. I have a feeling that something big is about to happen in my life; something is changing internally and externally. I am at a point in my life where I have little to lose or gain, so appearing a little foolish won't affect me one way or another.

I don't have to make excuses for my behavior. My personal history speaks for itself. I am what I am, but I might be more than you think. I for sure am not a child abuser. You know it and I know it. I am yet upset about the accusations. I hope settlement of this issue is in our near future. Anyway, let me get on with my task.

When I was a teenager, about fifteen, I believe. I hypnotized myself by lying face up on my bed while staring at a spot on the ceiling. I stared and stared at it until becoming myopic, then visually and mentally blank. That spot became the center of my universe. I had already created and collected a lifetime of mental movies about myself, and would then recall many of them while in this state of mind.

I presently do the same thing, but now with less intensity. It seems more natural and easy now, and not in any kind of hypnotic state. I now use them for different reasons. There are millions of movies in my head. I play them on demand for practical purposes these days, and for work and entertainment. I have been playing thousands of them as I write these letters, recalling our history.

I started young playing mental movies of my experiences. I originally played the mental movies for only entertainment, but later turned this behavior into a self-life study, a tool for remembering and an exercise for internal time travel.

Once putting myself in this visual and mental blank state, I regressed into personal life history archives. I played a movie of something that happened that day, and then one of something yesterday and then maybe one of a week ago. I continued playing the regressive experience movies back through time. Each movie took a short amount of time. I condensed and simplified them. I watched mental movies of a month ago, a year ago and so on until being a small child. I got far into my history only a few times. I reverted farther and farther a couple of times until finding myself in my mother's womb.

I finally took myself back to a point before birth. I was in heaven or some place of transition, in transition material becoming a baby, then a fetus and then a zygote. I regressed a few times until one day I found myself in trouble. I could not return to my ceiling, my bed or my room. I could not find my way back. I got scared and nearly panicked. I was stuck somewhere in darkness. I must have felt much like you felt when fighting to stay alive, desiring to get out of the womb. I finally did calm down and thoughtfully found my way back home, finally becoming conscious of my present time surroundings. I quit hypnotizing myself after that. I was afraid that I might not make it back the next time. I never went back to that place. I have been tempted many times to experience self-hypnosis again, but have not followed through.

When I was about thirty-five years old, I would Zen sit, counting breaths to ten repeatedly until I blanked my mind. I put myself into a state of nearly thoughtlessness. I could remain in that state for only a short time. There were too many distractions, even though I sat in a quiet place with legs crossed, palms up and eyes closed. Some influencing power took me to familiar and unfamiliar places.

I kept trying to reach "nirvana" with little to no success. I think I neared the edge of it for a moment one time. Supposedly, the original Buddha sat under a tree for sixteen years before reaching nirvana. Siddhartha learned about life from a river and a spiritual man who constantly smiled. Look up the book "Siddhartha." I know nearly nothing about Zen. Forgive my ignorance. I do think though, that one of the best places to reside is in ignorance, for there the so-called "real" world doesn't clutter or confuse. That old saying, "ignorance is bliss," is pretty much right except a person can't earn a living in that state of mind. Ignorance is a place of nothing and everything. I only got to the edge of that place a few times. I try to remain ignorant about several things. I yet sit non-ritually and erase my mind of clutter, allowing thought to flow and spirits to enter my mind. I frequently invite the Holy Spirit to enter my mind.

When I was in my forties, I tried staring into a large oval wall mirror by candle light in an effort to allow the spiritual world to enter my earthly world. I wished my mind to be a conduit for the spiritual world. I sat for hours several times and nothing happened. One time, however, I felt as if I was entering the mirror. I felt myself passing through the glass. It was smooth and soft and I didn't fear cutting of flesh. I thought I saw movement in the mirror for only a moment. I seemingly saw the constant blue cobalt eyes of the devil. I had no doubt to whom they belonged. They penetrated my mind for only a few seconds, but it was enough for me to leave the mirror place. I've always been tempted to go back to that place and experience the devil's lure, but haven't had the courage. I see that cobalt blue color everywhere these days, especially in electrical and electronic lights. I think many LED's are blue these days. I yet wish to flirt with the spiritual world, but am not so sure I want to enter it. I'm not sure I have the courage to see the positive and negative side of that world. I believe it is all around me. I live in it. I am part of it and don't really know it. I have a feeling that I am about to enter it whether I wish it or not. God help me if I am entering it now. I only want to experience the positive side of course, not the negative side, but I think it comes as a package. I am preparing to go there.

The last experience that I will write about was when I was in my fifties and at the pinnacle of my spirituality. It was after Kaitlyn died. I couldn't maintain the intensity. It was consuming for a little while and I was in a near constant spiritual state. I called myself a living prayer. The experience about which I write was after saying night prayers, and while remaining in a meditating state of mind. I opened my mind, soul and spirit to whoever wished to enter. I preferred the Holy Spirit. My relationship with Him was and is special. I was in a state of mind, a combination of Zen, hypnosis and prayer. I was teetering on the edge of that mysterious place having slightly been there before in different forms. I wished the spiritual world to come into me. I was opening myself, allowing what might happen to happen. I tried to ignore earthly influences. I gave myself up. My mind was nearly thoughtless, and then in an instant, something captured my full attention. Then a flash of light filled my eyes. I saw a partial view of Jesus' eye. It was a tiny glimpse, but like a silent stone, flying into my mind's eye. I saw only a slice of His clear brown iris and tiny pupil with perfect white surrounding. It was an overwhelming feeling that caught me by surprise. I instantly knew exactly what it was. I don't know how I knew. It was only a split second glance of

His eye and yet it caused streaming tears. I felt the power of His love for me. I could not withstand it but for a moment, and that was all that was offered. I couldn't describe then and cannot describe today the feeling I experienced. It was the taking of my soul for a moment. I felt myself falling onto my face and weeping. I couldn't say a word. I could hardly breathe. I could only prostrate myself before Him. All earthly feelings of love and passion were exhibiting within me. Christians call it, "agape love."

I will never forget that moment in that place, in that state of mind. I think if I had seen His complete eye, I would have died. It was that powerful. It was a thousand times more powerful than any place I've been, outside or inside myself. That glimpse changed me. I've lost much of its influence, but residual memories linger well in my soul. I play that mental movie every once in awhile. It taught me how much God loves and how little I love. I also learned how unimportant I am, and how small and useless I am. However, at the same time, I learned that Jesus does indeed love me. Now that is something to remember. I kept wishing to hear, "I accept you," but I'm sure that will have to wait.

I momentarily slip into that place often these days, provoked by external influences and internal emotions. I don't need hypnosis, Zen or smoke and mirrors. I have little control except for being available and willing to be spiritually touched. I'm wary of going back to that place for an absolute time no matter the mode. I'm afraid I will only go there for an extended time when I'm dead. That place is constantly beckoning me one way or another. I need to look for signs, listen for advice and seek influences that I can trust. I yet think something big is about to happen in my life. All I can do is wait.

Sincerely,

Dad

Water Pool

My life this moment is
like a small water pool,
motionless, reflecting light,
smooth as a mirror.
I look into its depths and
see what mind remembers.
Melancholy washes over me
like an ocean wave,
impossible in my pool, but
possible in my mind.
My heart aches for past
relationships, family and
children.
I can see my world
then and now.
I can feel my emotions
then and now.
I can smell and taste
my relationships
then and now.
I reach out and touch water,
causing it to ripple, and
my moment is gone.

Dear Angela – *Lack of Courage*

I stopped at the "Cross" located at Groom, Texas a second time when going up through New Mexico and Colorado to see Kristen. I had this feeling nearly all the way, while intentionally driving towards the giant cross, that I had a special mission. A description of my mission kept accumulating until it was a movie in my head. I got the notion that I was to heal someone there at the cross. I was to be a short-time angel and touch a crippled woman to remove her ailment. I would never know if I healed her or not, but would have to go on about my trip only having faith that I did the right thing. I kept playing the movie in my head and it seemed simple while driving towards Texas, but then it started getting complicated the closer I got to the cross.

I pulled into the parking area, got out of my truck and made my way around the circular stations depicting the crucifixion of Christ. I finally found myself sitting on a bench near the three crosses on the hill. I sat there for some time thinking and replaying the mission movie in my head. My confidence was waning with each minute sitting there waiting on the woman. I started to doubt if she would even appear. The whole thing began to seem rather stupid. I stood to return to my truck and behold a woman was slowly limping towards me. She got about ten feet away and stared me right in the eyes. We looked at each other for nearly ten seconds. It seemed a long time. It was as if she wished me to speak to her. She got about six feet away.

I started arguing with myself about touching or not touching her. My mind was ablaze. I could hardly think. The movie kept flashing in mind and my heart was pounding.

"All you have to do is shake her hand, touch her shoulder, do something," I encouraged myself.

I paused. I did nothing. Twenty seconds passed. A man, I assumed her husband, came to help her down the steps. "No, no, I can do it. I will catch-up," she said softly, then glanced at me one more time before turning away.

I stood and did nothing, said nothing. I admonished myself for lack of courage, for lack of faith. I sat back down and watched her shuffle along the sidewalk heading for the parking lot. I sat there for quite some time and finally headed for the parking area myself. I was nearly to my truck when I saw her getting into a van only four cars from my parking space. I had another chance, but now her family was present. I had no idea how to approach her. I again had no courage.

"Oh, what you must think of me, Lord," I whispered. "No wonder you hesitate giving me spiritual gifts."

I went on to my truck and drove away without fulfilling my mission. And, now I find myself in a similar place, not having the courage to confront you and your unfounded accusations. I don't have the courage to help you out of your predicament, your mental limp. I should do something to help you. I'm afraid time will pass and you will be getting in that van and driving away. I'm afraid if too much time passes, you will start to believe your lies and there will be no consequences, no mending. I'm afraid someday the lies will come back to haunt you. I need to have courage so that you will gain courage. I'm afraid you will turn from me, walk away and I will have done nothing to help heal your mental affliction or save you from possible further abuse.

Sincerely,

Dad

In a Granary No More

Words spoken
on a road to
nowhere are
meaningless.
Like a bent
quarter
won't spend or a
broken top
won't spin,
unfair words won't
correct.

Time tells secrets,
causes cracks and
faults that
chinking cannot repair.
Precious wheat
spilled from a
splintered granary
cannot speak,
for it has
no voice.

o

Your words are like
scattered wheat
escaping through
undiscovered faults.
You are being carried
windward, heading
somewhere unknown.
Wheat can speak and
make sense to
those hungry for lies.

So collect,
put in order and
save yourself for
you shall not
be here long.
You're on a
meaningful way
towards green
horizon and
golden somewhere,
alone.

o

You're not
in a granary
anymore,
enslaved by
cracks to survive,
getting wider with
time.
You are free,
carried away from a
black winged gusty
feast.

You're on a
defining life
path,
spinning
yarns and
blending
truth and lies,
while sun,
rain and

morning light
endure.

It's a long path
full of revelation.
You're destined for
consumption.
Only you can decide
whether becoming
simple food or
communion bread
served with wine.
You're in a granary
no more.

Dear Angela – *Debi's Letter to Angela*

Dear Angela, 12/31/2011

The snow has been deep this Christmas and it reminds me how much you loved the sledding. It has been quiet without you. We put up the tree, but things just weren't the same. Our lives have been sad and resigned since the summer. It has been particularly hard on your dad who loves you and misses you so much. Surely you must know how much we love you and how hard the last six months have been.

I hear from the girls that you are in school and seem to be enjoying your new life. They keep track of you on Facebook and let us know when you post important events and accomplishments. It would be wonderful to talk to you directly about your studies and your new adventures.

I find myself asking what prompted you to create the story of your dad abusing you. We have spent many hours trying to sort this all out. If you did not want to visit this summer because of your other commitments, we surely would have understood. You are growing up and have a great many things happening in your life. I worry that these lies will not only estrange you from the people that love you – but they will also create a burden on your conscience that will never be shaken. You should know that we love you unconditionally. No matter what you do or say, you will never alter the foundation of that love.

We are going to Florida for two months this year. This time we have rented a condo on the water. It will give us more room than that little travel trailer that we used last winter. We were really close in that small space – especially when the weather was cold! It might not have been the best experience for you – still, we were together as a family for a few days!

I am torn in writing this letter. The social service investigation up here was a horrible experience. If you are ever falsely accused of a crime you will know what this feels like. I pray that you never have to go through anything like this. Your dad wants to reach out to you, but feels torn, as well. How does one reconcile ones love for a daughter with the horrific details of a false story?

Over the past months your dad has written a book, Letters to Angela. This is a heart-felt tribute to you that tells a story from the time you were first glimpsed on the ultra-sound to the present day. I hope that someday you will be able to read it and understand just how much you mean to him.

I just want you to know that we love you and want you to be whole. Time goes by so quickly and we lose opportunities to share our feelings and our thoughts with each other. You are a special part of our lives and I love you as my own daughter. This will never change.

I hope that things are going well with your studies. It is hard to believe that you are already in college with a new set of friends and experiences. I also hope that you are having some fun with your horses this winter break.

We would love to hear from you.

Love,

Debi

Dear Angela – *First Contact Emails*

Included in this letter are your two short emails speaking to Debi and me that gave us hope. They caused us to believe that indeed your conscience is working and that you know you have done a very wrong thing. Even though, your response to Debi's letter sent 12/31/2011 was much less than we would have liked, it was a response. You used the word "complexity," but we have no idea what you're talking about and of course, that is your business.

Angela Reisner-Parn January 4, 2011 at 10:54pm

oh Debi if only you knew the complexity of this situation . . .
please know that i love you so so very much . . .
and one day i hope to explain

I need much more than the two words you sent to me, but I will gladly accept them for now. Thank you.

Angela Reisner-Parn January 4, 2011 at 10:55pm

love you

Lies always complicate any situation, and encourage more lies. Life is complex enough without complicating it more with lies. Sometimes we don't tell the truth and cut corners. Lies are like shortcuts that seem pragmatic at the time.

Do you remember not pronouncing Pythagorean Theorem correctly when first learning Geometry? Well, Pythagoras had it right mathematically about the areas of triangular areas and that theorem can go on and on, getting very complicated. I have especially been concerned about the hypotenuse, using it to find if something is square and true in construction.

I experienced the hypotenuse long before I knew about geometry. My dad taught me about the 3, 4 and 5 Pythagorean triple when I was ten years old. We constructed things on the farm and neither of us had learned geometry, but things had to be square and plumb. We used it for that purpose. It's strange how knowledge and wisdom is shared, and how a man with no formal education could teach me so much without my awareness.

Traveling the hypotenuse might be the shortest distance between two triangular points, but it's usually the most dangerous and there is a lot of area to consider along the way.

There are two sides to every story and the truth is usually some place in the middle. In our case, there is no middle. There is no shortcut to the truth. Your lies were like leaping the hypotenuse as if being a child without consideration for consequences. Your emails are an adult beginning to solving our problem.

We are yet here and love you "confetti" much.

Sincerely,

Dad

When I was Ten

I was invincible
when a boy
ten years old.
I could leap and
roll from
great heights.
Great heights being
six feet or less.
I ran, jumped and
rolled at
low heights and
gradually worked
my way up to
twelve glorious feet.
Towards a barn
loft door
I ran and
leaped from a
height of
twelve feet, and a
distance of
twelve feet.
I hypotenuse
arced with courage and
excitement.
I began turning
body before hitting
grassy earth with a
magnificent rolling,
painless thud.
I flew a
few times and
lived to
write about it
until

I got older,
bigger and
wiser.
I quit such
foolishness at
fourteen, but that
skill remains
buried within
my psyche,
just in case
I ever need
it as an adult.
Anything was yet
possible at
thirteen.
Everything turned
questionable at
eighteen.
And by thirty,
I forgot
how to leap,
fly and roll,
for there was
no hypotenuse
anymore beyond
mathematics.

Dear Angela – *Perspective*

I have been watching the news during the past few days. So very much of it has been concentrating on the shooting at Tucson, Arizona where congresswoman Giffords received a severe bullet wounding to the head, the killing of six other people including a nine-year-old girl and the wounding of many others by a twenty-two year old madman with a gun. It really had nothing to do with politics. His young mind was deranged and he had no grasp of reality.

The whole situation made me think about our lives, how blessed we are and that what you did, even though bad, was not nearly as horrible as we first thought and suggested. That situation put real perspective on our situation.

Sometimes the world, or possibly God, shows us that what is happening in our personal lives is not so bad. Of course, I constantly ask why God allows such things to happen and of course, I am left wanting for answers.

I am also reading the book *Valley Forge* by Newt Gingrich and am realizing how horrible George Washington and his army had it during the winter of 1777. I have read only three chapters, and at the end of the third chapter, George Washington is alone and is about to pray for divine guidance. I again have put our situation in perspective, realizing that those revolutionary soldiers had a horrible time. I read how horrible the war was and about hardship and death. The book is teaching me a lesson and I've barely started reading it.

I have also reflected again on Kaitlyn's passing, realizing again that our situation is not horrible, but her passing was horrible. I can only wait for what God has planned for us. I can only pray as George Washington prayed. He was guidance praying for 12,000 men. I am guidance praying for only you, Debi and me, and our plight is not life and death depending. We are yet blessed.

I look out through my glass wall of windows and doors onto the Carrabelle River Bay and see shrimp boats and other white pleasure craft anchored. I see birds of many species flying high and skimming the water, and dolphins swimming and occasionally surfacing for air. All is well here in my warm condominium with sixty-five-degree January temperature outside. All seems well, here with Debi, in our little safe world where I know you yet love us and we love you no matter what.

I can only wait to write the ending, or the last letter, of this last chapter. I can only wait to learn where my friend the Holy Spirit will lead me and what these letters will teach.

I can only ask, "What is going to happen to me?"

Sincerely,

Dad

My God Piece

With sweet remorse
I sit with chin
on hands,
resting thoughts,
resting day and
feeling melancholy.

Night sky seeks
my attention as
its moniker
fills soul, for
I fear darkness
sketching reality.

I fear that
I won't witness
equal tomorrow for
time is making
enemies in
my body.

Aging is time's
abiding partner and
yet I think and
remember as if a
young man of
twenty-five.

In foolish
recollections,
tomorrow will
enlighten for
my soul will
never fade.

I know my spirit is
wafting towards
where I began as
weightless thoughts
beguile
vulnerable faith.

My God piece
speaks and
morning light flows
freely in my aware
essence recalling
mystical home.

Oh, sweet remorse
you fold hands in
prayer, and place
earthly brain and
body into heavenly
mind and soul.

Dear Angela – *Forgiveness*

Sometimes forgiveness is a hard pill to swallow. I certainly don't like the taste of it. I have always tried to think myself through a situation so that I personally would not have to apologize. I have also tried not to put others in a position, whereby, feeling compelled to lie. Of course lying is always an option for some people, according to their particular assessment of circumstances.

I'm not good at forgiving big things. It's good that big things seldom come along in life. I am wrestling with the whole idea of forgiveness; of course, I intellectually know exactly what it means, but am having trouble in my heart feeling what it means. In the heart is the most important place to understand forgiveness. I can say, "I'm sorry" easily, but find it hard to say, " Forgive me." Does that make sense to you? I think it is even harder to say, "I forgive you." You see, this whole subject of forgiveness is complicated. Is that what you meant by "complex" in your email or are you talking about your circumstances?

Forgiveness seems to be a life circle of confession, repentance and penalty; whereby it takes at least two parties to draw the circle. I seek none of the above for I have no need for them.

I think forgiveness is between oneself and God if the perpetrator of wrongdoing. I also think it is between the perpetrated and God. Forgiveness for earthly beings is small in comparison to heavenly forgiveness. I don't need you to say, "Forgive me." I thought I needed that in the beginning, but not now. It is a new year, January 29, and a new beginning. Forgiveness is not important to me. I will love you no matter what. I can forget wrong doing and pretend it never happened, but I think you will have to tell the truth to those around you. I am happy. Truth and confidence are the foundation for happiness.

Mahatma Gandhi said, "We must become the change we want to see." I am yet changing and growing into what I want to see in myself.

Sincerely,

Dad

Situation Heaviness

World weight sits on
my shoulders.
I feel it down
past feet into earth.
My muscles ache as
mind seeks tomorrow.
I wish I could
sleep tonight.
When did I accept
liability or did
I have a choice?
I am no weight lifter.
I am no genius
about weights and
measurement.
I am only a foolish man
wishing to be left alone.
I think, however,
my being here and
being a human being,
makes me a responsible
weight lifter and an
accommodating student of
situation load.

Pick Me

Oh, Holy Spirit,
pick me to do
your work.
Elevate me to
your shoulders
so that I might
see tomorrow.
Lower me to
my knees
so that I might
know true humility.
Transport me
on truth and
confident light to
heaven and
back for
wisdom's sake.
I ask,
"Why not me?"
Earthly time is
short.
My soil is
yet fertile.
I await
your hand upon
my shoulder.

Dear Angela – *Your Room*

I walked into your room at our house today and looked around, seeing evidence of you everywhere. I looked at your furniture and remembered buying it while living at Jenny's farm. I wonder if you will want it someday. It's white and has flowers painted on the headboard and drawer fronts. Maybe you have outgrown it. I guess you could paint over the flowers. Everyone loves to sleep in that warm waterbed during the winter months.

I looked at the walls and saw pictures representing your history. I also looked in the closet and saw all those games, puzzles and toys. Do you think you will want any of them? I wonder if you will sleep in that bed ever again. I looked in the drawers and saw all kinds of objects including art supplies and papers.

I felt sad in that room. I remembered staying there until you went to sleep because of being afraid of having bad dreams. I remembered looking past the ajar door watching you sleep. I remembered waking you in the morning, but most of all, I remembered hugging and saying goodnight to you.

That room is yet a special place for me. Your life stuff is yet there waiting for someone or something. The future of that stuff is as tenuous as your future, except it can do nothing to promote itself, unlike dynamic you, who has the world waiting for your influence and courageous touch.

Sincerely,

Dad

Dear Angela – *Last Letter*

It is hard to believe that I have not talked to you in a year and have not seen you in nearly one and a half years. I have been waiting patiently for something big to happen in my life, but it has not. I now wait as small changes happen in my life.

I sit by my Wabash River listening, watching as it pushes outward past banks, as floodwaters seem to have a mind of their own. The river has a mind of its own. I have a mind of my own. I can nearly hear the river speak. I can nearly hear the Holy Spirit speak, Kaitlyn speak and you speak. Celestial advice is but a retrospective moment away and I cannot grasp it.

I continue to wait as small life changes occur and I grow older and hopefully wiser. I continue to listen . . .

CONCLUSION

I see Angela as wind pushed, rain-washed and spirit influenced. I wish she could read her own scrapbook collected words and see her own scrapbook displayed pictures. Our history is a wonderful story. She came up with the expression to describe how much she loved me. It is somewhat silly, but we knew exactly what it meant. I wish she would remember saying, "I love you confetti much."